Christmas in Washington

Cook Book

by

Janet Walker

GOLDEN
WEST ☼
PUBLISHERS

Cover photo courtesy Chamber of Commerce, Leavenworth, WA

Printed in the United States of America

ISBN #1-885590-07-5

First Printing

Golden West Publishers, Inc.
4113 N. Longview Ave.
Phoenix, AZ 85014, USA
(602) 265-4392

Christmas in Washington Cook Book

Table of Contents

Washington at a Glance

Size — 20th largest state in area
Statehood — November 11, 1889, the 42nd state
Highest Elevation — Mount Rainier—14,410'
Lowest Elevation — Pacific Ocean, sea level
Highest Temp. to Date — 118 degrees, lowest is -48
Farmland — 16,000,000 acres
Named for: — George Washington
State Flag — Green with picture of George Washington
State Motto — "Alki", an Indian word meaning "bye and bye"
State Nickname — "The Evergreen State"
State Bird — Willow Goldfinch (or Wild Canary)
State Fruit — Apple
State Tree — Western Hemlock
State Flower — The Coast Rhododendron
State Gem — Petrified wood
State Fish — Steelhead trout

Acknowledgements

The author and the publisher would like to express their appreciation for the wonderful recipes, comments and cooperation received from the Washington cooks and companies who contributed to this book:

Annette Wilkins	Grace Ingvarsson	Mary Will Price
Albatross B & B	James House	Vera Rome
Iona Durnan	Jennifer Knudson	Salish Lodge
Bernice Dye	Margie's Inn on the Bay	Shelburne Inn
Joan Dye	Betsy Mastalski	Jean Sherman
Joyce Fowler	Lucille McDaniel	Simone's Groveland
Patricia Fowler	June McGlothlin	Cottage B&B
Fulton House	Mio Amore Pensione	Rebecca Smith
Betty Frain	Moon and Sixpence	Ann Starrett Mansion
Willa Godinez	Mt. Rainier Guest Serv.	Marilyn Tatham
Marena Hall	Florence Nesseim	Turtleback Farm Inn
Harbinger Inn	North Garden Inn	Jerry Walker
Jana Hawkins	Ocean Crest Resort	Jim Walker
Evelyn Hayes	Stephanie Osborne	Lisa Walker
Jimmie Holeman	Marcia Pepperworth	Opal Watson
Lois Holeman	Bill Peterson	Marie Webb

Introduction

There's no place like home for the Holidays! Whether it's turkey or ham with all the trimmings, candied yams, cranberry salads—it's a time for all of our traditional favorites. This is an appropriate moment to reflect on the spirit of the season and the importance of friends and family, a time to sing carols, wrap gifts, and decorate trees with cherished ornaments.

Our state is a melting pot of the many nationalities that have become a part of our heritage. This book contains many family holiday favorites. Some of the recipes have a rich and lengthy history. Others are of more recent descent. All of the recipes have one thing in common. They are a wonderful addition to any holiday gathering. Try the many diverse ethnic favorites and discover new tastes, savory delights and traditions for your family!

Christmas in Washington is strolling down a snowy street in the bustling village of Leavenworth. It is meandering down a winding path while marvelling at the thousands of Christmas lights of the Tacoma zoo or gazing for hours as the boats with their holiday decorations pass by in Seattle.

Christmas in our state is the observation of the many customs of the peoples who have come to be citizens here.

So, decorate your door with a festive wreath. Then open it wide and welcome family and friends to share the magic that this holiday brings.

Christmas in Washington Celebrations

Throughout the Evergreen State, many cities celebrate Christmas in their own way. Although we could not possibly list them all, you are cordially invited to enjoy Washington's festivities!

ANACORTES: **Christmas Parade, Lighted Ships Parade,** second weekend in December. The Lions Club goes all out in presenting its daytime Christmas Parade. In the evenings watch the lighted ships parade.

ANACORTES: **Tree Lighting, Artwalk,** early December. This All-American City welcomes everyone to its Christmas tree lighting. Downtown merchants host Artwalk, and local Bed and Breakfast's have an open house the next day.

BELLINGHAM: **International Creche Festival,** late November through January 1. Browse among the more than 50 store windows in the downtown area as they display over 1,000 nativity sets from around the world.

BELLINGHAM: **Holiday Port Festival and Lighted Boat Parade,** early December. This event is geared toward children with musical entertainment, dance groups, an orchestra, dog sled and fire engine rides and a Santa scene. The lighted boat parade on Bellingham Bay is held on the second Sunday of December.

BIRCH BAY: **Polar Bear Swim,** January 1. Are these people crazy....or what? They're braving the chilly waters of beautiful Birch Bay in mid-Winter, but they seem to be having a great time ushering in the New Year. Prizes, hot drinks and chili.

CHELAN: **Victorian Holidays,** early December. A 1902 Victorian mansion is all decked out for the holidays so you can shop for top quality arts and crafts, and listen to the Dickens carolers at the Highland Guest House.

CHEWELAH: **Festival of Lights,** first two weekends in December. Throughout the city park and downtown, the holiday lights abound. Have fun chugging around town with Santa aboard the Chewelah Choo-Choo mini-train, and visit the Winter Craftfest.

COLVILLE: **Keller House Candlelight Tours,** early December. The 1910 Keller House gets all spruced up in old-fashioned decorations for your enjoyment. Next door is a museum which is also decorated.

COSMOPOLIS: **Dickens Family Christmas,** early December. One of the largest craft shows you'll ever see. High tea with Queen Victoria or dinner with the Cratchets.

FREELAND: **Kris Kringle Fest,** early December. Take a ferry to Whidbey Island and join the Kris Kringle Fire Engine Brigade Parade. This is small town America at its best, as the whole town joins in caroling at the local mall.

GRANGER: **Granger Berry Patch,** December weekends. In the lower Yakima Valley here's a chance to relive your childhood with an old-fashioned hayride to cut your own Christmas tree. Hot chocolate and cookies along the way!

ILWACO: **Cranberry Festival.** Continuous entertainment highlights this pre-holiday festival on the north side of the Columbia River. There are craft and food vendors, and the museum cafe features cranberry goodies. Tour the cranberry bogs to watch berry harvesting in progress. Finish it off by watching the Cranberry Follies, an old time vaudeville show.

ISSAQUAH: **Santa's Reindeer Farm,** early December to Christmas. There's a whole herd of reindeer at the Washington Zoological Park for the kids to visit, and even the jolly old elf himself.

LA CONNER: **Lighted Land Yacht and Christmas Boat Parade,** early December. Here's a lighted RV parade and also a boat parade as Santa comes to town.

LEAVENWORTH: **Leavenworth Lighting Festival,** first two weekends in December. A magical winter wonderland as this Bavarian-themed town comes to life each year. Join thousands of people crowded onto Main Street in front of the bandstand, as everyone sings "Silent Night". Then, the countdown begins. As the count reaches 1...the Christmas lights of the entire city burst into brightness. There's oom-pah-pah music from the bandstand, a snowman contest, sleigh rides, delicious Bavarian food and of course, Mr. and Mrs. Claus.

LYNDEN: **Sinterklaas Celebration,** early December. The Dutch heritage of Lynden comes alive as Sinterklaas appears on a white horse with his elfin helper, Piet.

MONTESANO: **Festival of Lights,** second weekend in December. A small town aglow with holiday lights, luminarias and an evening grand parade. There's even a Jingle Bell Jog, a singing Christmas tree, a live nativity scene and old Santa, too!

PASCO: **Annual Holiday Lighting,** early December. At one of the Tri-Cities largest wineries, you're invited to celebrate with thousands of lights throughout the vineyards and tasting room. Entertainment, food and wine.

PORT ANGELES: **Festival of Trees,** late November. Many trees decorated in a variety of themes highlight this fund raiser for a local hospital. Attend a Friday night auction of the trees and enjoy dinner and dancing.

PORT ORCHARD: **Nautical Christmas Lane,** early December. Bring your camera, because photo moments are fantastic at this lighted boat competition. The public pier is the scene for this event.

PORT TOWNSEND: **B&B Christmas Open Parlor,** second weekend in December. Here's your opportunity to tour a number of decorated bed and breakfast parlors in this historic city by the Sound.

POULSBO: **Yule Fest,** early December. The Lucia Bride is escorted ashore as Vikings arrive by boat in this city on the shores of Puget Sound. Torch light parade and yule log lighting ceremony.

PUYALLUP: **A Victorian Country Christmas,** late November to early December. More than 400 Victorian shops create a festive indoor shopping area. Merchants are dressed in authentic Victorian costumes. Strolling musicians and cartoon characters for the kids to enjoy. A Living Nativity and Sugar Plum Theatre.

QUINCY TO GEORGE: **Lighted Christmas Scenes**, late November to January 1. This trip takes you past more than 20 Christmas scenes in lights and motion as you travel State Route 281 and Interstate 90.

SEATTLE: **Christmas Parade of Boats,** early December. An event all of Seattle awaits each year as this 21-day festival starts. Gaily decorated, the Spirit of Seattle leads the parade with on-board carolers as other decorated boats follow. Join in a bonfire party along the shore as the fire builders sing carols.

SEQUIM: **Christmas Season Fair,** early December. Chestnuts roasting on the open fire, Jack Frost nipping at your nose, music, hot spiced cider and wine are all a part of this festivity. The fair has lots of craft booths, too!

SUNNYSIDE: **Lighted Farm Implement Parade,** early December. Here's a twist: tractors, combines, swathers, grape pickers and other farm equipment are gaily lighted to represent Sunnyside's Country Christmas theme.

TACOMA: **Zoolights,** December 1 to 31. No one has counted how many lights are strung here, but it is said to be almost half a million. They bring a world of magical creatures to life as you stroll through Point Defiance Park Zoo. Just imagine over 150 zoo animals, landmarks and nursery rhymes in lights.

TENINO: **Winterfest in Historic Tenino,** early December. Hop on a horse-drawn wagon, travel back to the 19th century and enjoy the arts and crafts displays. A gingerbread house contest, food, entertainment and much more.

TOPPENISH: **Western Christmas Lighted Parade**, early December. Horse and mule drawn wagons pass by the Western-themed murals on downtown stores. Festively lighted and decorated, they draw a huge crowd to this rodeo city on the edge of the Yakima Indian Reservation.

TRI-CITIES: **Christmas Lighted Boat Parade,** early December. Watch Christmas-lighted boats as they cruise down the Columbia River.

VANCOUVER: **Evening of Treasures,** early December. Enjoy free carriage rides, a tree lighting, and a concert. Special holiday shopping, dining and entertainment.

VANCOUVER: **Fort Vancouver Celebration,** second weekend in December. Something a little bit different as costumed interpreters help you experience a pioneer Christmas, through period music and demonstrations.

WALLA WALLA: **Christmas Lighting Tour**, mid-December. In this town that is said to be named twice, (so you wouldn't forget the name), holiday spirits come alive as you join the tour of beautiful lights, amusing tour guides, holiday tunes and more!

YAKIMA VALLEY: **Thanksgiving in Wine Country,** late November. More than 20 wineries present their special fare with food and recipes too.

Call each city's Chamber of Commerce for more information about these special occasions.

Chapter One

Scandinavian Legacies

Christmas in Washington is a time of wonder and joy. While Washingtonians celebrate their global heritage throughout the year, many nationalities enjoy traditional feasts and festivals in December.

For example, Swedish families mark the darkest day of winter, December 13, as Santa Lucia Day, (the promise of Spring to come). This day is celebrated with the eldest daughter dressed in white (as the queen of lights). Wearing a red sash around her waist and a crown of pine boughs lighted with seven candles, she awakens her parents early on the morning of December 13 by singing, "Santa Lucia".

If there is a second eldest daughter, she carries a candle, wears a white robe, and places tinsel in her hair. The eldest son wears a pointed cap with silver stars, and a white robe. Lucia brings "lussekatter" (*Lucia Buns*—see recipe on next page) and coffee. The charming community of Poulsbo, on the shores of Puget Sound, holds its Yule Fest each year in celebration of this delightful tradition.

Scandinavians particularly like the smorgasbord type of dining. If you toured farm homes in Sweden, you would likely find a different meatball recipe in every kitchen, with each cook believing her version to be the very best. Our version, *Authentic Swedish Meatballs*, can be found on page 57.

Lutfisk, (also spelled lutefisk) is a Scandinavian specialty made from salted dry cod. See *Lutfisk* on page 56.

Christmas is a day of great feasting in Washington's Norwegian homes. Their tables groan with food, sporting great selections of cookies and breads. A favorite Christmas bread recipe for *Yule Kage* can be found on page 70.

All in all, a Scandinavian style Christmas offers a multitude of taste tempting treats.

Lucia Buns

1 tsp. saffron threads
1/4 cup boiling water
1 3/4 cups milk
5 tbs. butter
1 cup sugar
1 tsp. salt
1/2 cup lukewarm water
2 tsp. sugar
2 pkgs. active dry yeast

1 egg
7 cups unbleached all-purpose flour
1/2 cup blanched slivered almonds
1/2 cup candied orange and lemon
   peel, diced
2/3 cup golden raisins
1 egg beaten with 1 tsp. water
dark raisins for "cats eyes"

Soak saffron in boiling water and set aside. In saucepan, combine milk and butter over medium heat until very warm. Stir in the sugar and salt. Cook to lukewarm. Combine warm water and sugar and sprinkle over yeast mixture to dissolve.

In electric mixer bowl, beat egg and add yeast mixture, saffron threads and saffron water. Gradually add 1/2 of the flour (sifted). Beat for five minutes. Gradually add the balance of the flour adding the full amount only as needed to keep dough from being sticky. Turn dough onto lightly floured board, and knead until smooth and elastic. (8 to 10 minutes). Gently work in almonds, fruit peel and raisins, distributing evenly. Place in greased bowl, turning to grease top of dough. Cover with plastic wrap and let rise in warm place until doubled in bulk. Punch dough down.

Divide dough into 27 pieces (about 2 1/2 oz. ea.) Roll each piece into 10-inch strip. Form into S-shapes, coiling ends inward. Place on greased baking sheets two inches apart. Cover with kitchen towel and let rise in warm place until doubled in size.

Brush with egg-water mixture. Press two raisins into the top of each and bake at 350 degrees for about 15 minutes. Cool on wire rack.

Appetizers & Beverages

Scandinavian Meatballs

"Makes a lovely, hot appetizer for the Christmas holiday season. Wonderful to serve guests, just pop into a chafing dish and let guests serve themselves."—Iona Durnan, Yakima

1/3 cup ONION, diced
2 Tbsp. BUTTER, melted
1 lb. GROUND BEEF
1 cup MASHED POTATOES, unseasoned
1/3 cup DRY BREAD CRUMBS
1 Tbsp. FRESH PARSLEY, diced
1 tsp. SALT
1 EGG
1/4 cup WHIPPING CREAM
2 Tbsp. BUTTER, melted
2 Tbsp. OIL
2 Tbsp. FLOUR
1/4 tsp. ALLSPICE
1/2 tsp. KITCHEN BOUQUET®
1 1/2 cups WHIPPING CREAM
FRESH PARSLEY, chopped, garnish

Sauté onion in butter in small skillet until tender, set aside. Combine ground beef, potatoes, bread crumbs, parsley, salt, egg, 1/4 cup of whipping cream and sautéed onion. Mix until well blended; shape into 3/4 inch meatballs. Cover and chill at least one hour. Brown several meatballs at a time (until all are done) in combined butter and oil in a heavy skillet. Shake pan back and forth frequently; add more oil if needed. Remove meatballs as browned, and place in 2 qt. casserole. Keep hot in 200 degree oven. Pour off all but 2 Tbsp. of the pan drippings; stir in flour, allspice and kitchen bouquet. Cook one minute, stirring constantly. Remove from heat. Slowly stir in balance of whipping cream. Cook over low heat until slightly thickened. Pour over meatballs, garnish with parsley.

Hot Chili Dip

"Our Christmas traditions were not much different from others, except for the menu. When I was a little girl, my grandparents would come to visit us in their 1933 Hudson. We would make homemade peppermint ice cream together. After dinner, we would sit with our feet in the warm oven of the wood stove as we ate our ice cream"—Annette Wilkins, Bellingham

1 lg. can HOT TAMALES
BUTTER
2 cloves GARLIC
1 lg. ONION, grated
1 lg. can CHILI WITHOUT BEANS
2 dashes TABASCO®
SEASONING SALT or SALT, to taste
1 lb. SHARP CHEDDAR CHEESE, grated

Mash tamales. In butter, sauté garlic and onion in heavy skillet until golden. Add chili, tabasco, and salt; combine with mashed tamales. Add grated cheese; heat and serve with chips for dipping.

Barbecue Cups

3/4 lb. GROUND BEEF
1/4 cup ONIONS, diced
2 Tbsp. BROWN SUGAR
1/2 cup BARBECUE SAUCE
1 can (10 oz.) REFRIGERATOR BISCUITS
3/4 cup CHEDDAR CHEESE, grated

Preheat oven to 400 degrees. Brown beef and drain. Add onion, brown sugar and barbecue sauce. Place biscuits in ungreased muffin tins; press dough to cover bottom and sides. Spoon mixture into each cup; sprinkle with cheese. Bake 10 to 12 minutes.

Smoked Duck Turnover

1 cup WILD MUSHROOMS, diced small
3/4 cup RIESLING WINE
1 lb. SMOKED DUCK MEAT, shredded
1 cup DUCK DEMI-GLACE
10 RYE BREAD SLICES
1 cup EGG WASH (1 EGG, 2 Tbsp. WATER)

Sauté mushrooms; deglaze with wine. Reduce by 3/4 and add demi-glace, remove from heat. Add duck meat, and refrigerate. Punch out 3 inch rounds from bread slices, reserve trimmings and process into fresh bread crumbs using food processor. Place approximately 1 1/2 ounces of duck filling in the center of each bread circle. Brush edges with egg wash, fold bread in half over filling and press edges together. Crimp with fork to seal edges. Brush sealed turnovers with egg wash and coat with seasoned bread crumbs. Pan fry to golden brown and keep warm in oven. Serve with cold **Fig Relish**.

Fig Relish

2 lbs. FIGS, fresh, small, diced
1/2 lb. ONION
3 cloves GARLIC, minced
1/2 cup SHERRY
1/2 cup HONEY
2 oz. BALSAMIC VINEGAR
1 BAY LEAF
1 Tbsp. BLACK PEPPERCORNS, cracked
1 lb. PEARS, diced
2 tsp. LEMON ZEST, grated
1/2 cup MINT, fresh chopped

Combine all ingredients, except last three. Simmer on low heat for 30 minutes, add pears. Continue to simmer 15 minutes, finish with remaining ingredients and cool.

Cheddar Cheese Puffs with a Surprise

"A must for those impromptu Holiday guests. Especially nice arranged on a platter of cheeses or fruit."—Stephanie Osborne, Puyallup

2 cups SHARP CHEDDAR CHEESE, grated
1 cube BUTTER, room temperature
1 cup FLOUR, sifted
1/2 tsp. SALT
1/2 tsp. PAPRIKA
48 sm. GREEN STUFFED OLIVES, well drained

Preheat oven to 400 degrees. Blend cheese and butter; stir in flour, salt and paprika. Mold 1 tsp. of the mixture around each olive; chill puffs until firm (about 30 minutes). Arrange on ungreased baking sheet and bake 15 minutes or until brown. (You can freeze the puffs well wrapped for about 10 days, then bake still frozen until browned.)

Holiday Artichoke Dip

1 lg. can ARTICHOKE HEARTS (packed in water)
1 cup MAYONNAISE
3 oz. CREAM CHEESE, softened
3/4 cup PARMESAN CHEESE

Blend all ingredients and heat for about 20 minutes at 350 degrees. Serve with chips, crackers or raw vegetables.

Wassail Punch

1 cup GRAPEFRUIT JUICE
2 1/2 cups ORANGE JUICE
2 cups APPLE CIDER
1/2 cup WATER
1/4 cup SUGAR
6 whole CLOVES
1 CINNAMON STICK, broken

Combine juices, cider and water in a large kettle. Stir in sugar and spices. Heat slowly until mixture is ready to boil. Strain spices and serve from a large punch bowl. If you prefer, add 1 1/2 cups of your favorite spirits.

Hot Mulled Wine

1 liter dry RED TABLE WINE
2 CINNAMON STICKS,
   broken in half
1 tsp. ALLSPICE

1 tsp NUTMEG
1 tsp. CLOVES
1 tsp. GINGER
ORANGE SLICES

Add spices to wine and heat over low heat until almost boiling. Serve in a punch glass with a slice of orange.

Rum Stone Sour

1 1/2 oz. ORANGE JUICE
1 1/2 oz. LEMON JUICE
1 Tbsp. SUGAR
1 1/2 oz. RUM, or your favorite spirits

Blend all ingredients and serve on the rocks in an old-fashioned cocktail glass. Serves one.

Chapter Two

O Christmas Tree . . .

It is said that Martin Luther, a German religious leader, began the custom of decorating trees way back in 1530. Trees were often decorated with apples, and called "Paradise Trees" representing Adam and Eve.

Later, the trees were decorated with paper roses outside in the town square. But it didn't take long for the ever-practical Germans to decide that freezing outdoors was not much fun, so they brought the tree inside.

Soon every family had a tree in the parlor. Decorations such as jewelry, mirrors, cotton, wool, handcrafted ornaments, and even silver knives and forks, were used. The trees were generally small and placed on a table covered with cloth. Gifts were arranged beneath.

In some homes, only the top of a large tree was cut, and then it was hung upside down in the doorway and decorated. It is easy to see why this custom didn't catch on.

Then, as now, many ornaments were handed down from generation to generation and became very treasured. Each year, one or two items were added to the collection.

In the United States, we tended to get bigger trees, hefty floor models with stands. And, for decorations, we branched out into all sorts of things. There were permanent works of art, and handcrafted ornaments of myriad shapes and sizes.

The Christmas tree has become a national symbol in the

United States. Many states (along with Washington) vie for the honor of supplying the White House with the national tree each year.

When it comes to selecting a tree, choices include artificial, fresh-cut, or rooted. Although artificial trees are cleaner and represent a one-time investment many families in the Northwest prefer a fresh-cut tree, with its fresh pine aroma and unique individuality.

There are many types of evergreens from which to choose, such as the long-needled Scotch pine, or maybe the short-needled Douglas fir. The Evergreen State has many types of home-grown trees available for the Christmas season.

Purchasing rooted trees is also becoming a treasured tradition, as trees can be planted to create permanent reminders of Christmases past.

Whatever kind of tree you choose for your holiday celebrations, always be sure that the tree does not become too dry and therefore a fire hazard.

We all know that evergreen boughs make beautiful wreaths. The Advent wreath custom begins the first Sunday in December and lasts till Christmas. This time is normally spent fasting and praying, while waiting for the celebration of the birth of Christ. Four red candles are encircled, each of which represents a Sunday of Advent. On each Sunday evening, a candle is burned, until all four candles are lit on Christmas Eve.

The Advent calendar is another German tradition. Starting on December 1 and ending on Christmas Eve, 24 numbered doors, windows, roofs, trees or boxes are opened, one each day. Children delight in the surprises awaiting them, which might be tempting sweets, or a keepsake or maybe a treasured scene.

The Bavarian village of Leavenworth (see cover photograph) teaches us much about the German customs, foods and music with its annual Christmas events which are attended by thousands from all parts of the state.

Holiday foods with Germanic influences are robust and flavorful. Sauerkraut and dumplings are staples of German cuisine. Try the *Chicken and Herb Dumplings* on page 58. You may appreciate the German version of Won Ton soup, *Moushella*, on page 36. The recipe for one of the most famous German desserts, *Bavarian Apple Strudel*, is on page 83.

Wish your friends a
Merry Christmas in German . . .

Froehliche Weihnachten!

Salads

Poached Pears

"A great recipe for winter when you rely so heavily on apples and pears. Always good to have a recipe that tastes great and is so pretty to look at."—Carol McGough. James House, Port Townsend

4 med. PEARS, slightly ripened
4 oz. LIGHT CREAM CHEESE
1 Tbsp. HONEY
1/4 tsp. VANILLA
2 Tbsp. VANILLA FLAVORED YOGURT (optional)
POWDERED SUGAR, for garnish
FRESH NUTMEG, for garnish

Cut pears in half, remove seeds and stem. Place pears cut side down in 9 x 13 baking pan, covered with 1/2 inch water. Bake at 350 degrees, for 20 to 30 minutes depending upon pear ripeness. Remove pears, place on glass serving dish, cut side up. Let cool. Soften cream cheese; mix with honey and vanilla until smooth. If smoother texture is desired, add yogurt. Place 1 Tbsp. of cream cheese mixture in center of each pear half; spoon 1 to 2 Tbsp. of **Rhubarb Sauce** over each half. Garnish with powdered sugar and fresh nutmeg.

Rhubarb Sauce

10 med. stalks RHUBARB, cut into 1/2 in. pieces
1 to 2 cups WATER
1 cup SUGAR
1 tsp. NUTMEG, fresh ground is best
RASPBERRIES, optional

Place cut rhubarb in medium size sauce pan with water (which should cover 50% of rhubarb when in pan). Bring to boil; stir in sugar. Cover saucepan and turn off heat. Let pan stay on burner until cool; add raspberries, if desired, for a brighter color. After sauce cools, stir thoroughly and add more sugar and nutmeg to taste.

Pretzel Salad

2 cups PRETZEL STICKS, crushed
3/4 cup BUTTER, melted
2 Tbsp. SUGAR
1 pkg. (8 oz.) CREAM CHEESE
1 pkg. (8 oz.) WHIPPED TOPPING
1 cup SUGAR
2 cups BOILING WATER
1 pkg. (6 oz.) STRAWBERRY GELATIN
2 pkgs. (10 oz.) FROZEN STRAWBERRIES

Prepare crust from first three ingredients and press down smooth and flat in a 9 x 13 inch pan. Bake at 400 degrees for 8 to 10 minutes, cool. (Do not use until completely cool.) Blend together cream cheese, topping and sugar until spreadable. Spread over crust; seal all edges. In boiling water, dissolve gelatin; add strawberries and stir until broken apart. Pour over cream cheese mixture and refrigerate.

Holiday Salmon Mold

1 Tbsp. PLAIN GELATIN
1 Tbsp. COLD WATER
1/2 cup BOILING WATER
1 can (16 oz.) SALMON, drained, flaked
1 cup reduced fat MAYONNAISE
1/2 cup diced CELERY

Combine gelatin and cold water. Add boiling water and stir until dissolved. Refrigerate until cold and syrupy. Add remaining ingredients and mix well. Turn into mold and chill until firm. Unmold on crisp salad greens, slice and serve.

Favorite Cranberry Salad

"In years past, I cut the cranberries by hand. Since my sister gave me a food chopper it has become my life sentence to make the cranberry salad for our family each Christmas."—Jerry Walker, Bellingham

1 lb. CRANBERRIES, ground
1 cup SUGAR
1 can (20 oz.) CRUSHED PINEAPPLE
1 lb. MARSHMALLOWS, cut into quarters
1 pt. WHIPPING CREAM

Mix cranberries and sugar together and let sit overnight. Combine crushed pineapple and marshmallows together, and let them sit overnight separately. The next day, combine the mixtures; mix well. Whip the cream and combine. If you freeze the cranberries, they will grind with very little mess. You need to be sure you have 16 oz. of cranberries and marshmallows, not just the 12 oz. packages. This is an exceptional salad for Christmas and Thanksgiving.

Christmas Pea Salad

2 cups CELERY, chopped
1 bunch GREEN ONIONS, chopped
1 pkg. (10 oz.) FROZEN PEAS, thawed
1/3 cup STUFFED GREEN OLIVES, chopped
1/4 cup RED BELL PEPPER, diced
2 sm. cans SHOESTRING POTATOES
MAYONNAISE, to moisten

One hour before serving, combine all ingredients except potatoes and mayonnaise; chill. Just before serving add potatoes and mayonnaise.

Egg Nog Cranberry Salad

"This is pretty in a glass pan. Enjoy!"—Marcia Pepperworth, Ferndale

1 pkg. (3 oz.) VANILLA PUDDING MIX
1 pkg. (3 oz.) LEMON FLAVORED GELATIN
2 cups WATER
2 Tbsp. LEMON JUICE
1 (3 oz.) RASPBERRY FLAVORED GELATIN
1 cup BOILING WATER
1 can (16 oz.) WHOLE CRANBERRY SAUCE
1/2 cup CELERY, finely chopped
1/4 cup PECANS, chopped
1 env. DESSERT TOPPING MIX
1/2 tsp. GROUND NUTMEG

In sauce pan, combine pudding mix, lemon gelatin and water. Cook and stir until mixture boils; stir in lemon juice and chill until partially set. Dissolve raspberry gelatin in boiling water; cook and stir until dissolved. Beat in cranberry sauce; fold in celery and nuts. Chill until partially set. Prepare dessert topping according to directions; add nutmeg and fold into pudding mixture. Pour half of pudding into 8 x 8 x 2 inch pan. Carefully pour cranberry layer over pudding, top with remaining pudding. Chill 6 hours or overnight.

O Christmas Tree . . .

O Christmas Tree, O Christmas tree
How lovely are your branches.
In summer sun, in winter snow,
A dress of green you always show.
O Christmas tree, O Christmas tree,
How lovely are your branches.

O Christmas tree, O Christmas tree,
With happiness we greet you,
When decked with candles once a year,
You fill our hearts with Yuletide cheer.
O Christmas tree, O Christmas tree,
With happiness we greet you.

Green Christmas Salad

"I like to serve a red and green salad for Christmas dinner because they look very festive on the table."—Florence Nesseim, Everett

1 pkg. (3 oz.) LIME GELATIN
1 1/2 cups HOT WATER
1 cup WHIPPING CREAM, whipped
1 cup COTTAGE CHEESE
1 sm. can CRUSHED PINEAPPLE
NUT MEATS
1/2 cup MARASCHINO CHERRIES, cut up

Combine gelatin and water; let set until slightly thickened. Beat with an electric mixer 1-2 minutes on low. Whip cream and mix the two together. Add cottage cheese, pineapple, nut meats and cherries. Let set overnight.

Festive Salad

2 cups shredded GREEN CABBAGE
2 cups shredded RED CABBAGE
2 cups shredded RAW CARROTS
1 cup RAISINS
1/2 cup chopped ALMONDS
3/4 to 1 cup reduced fat MAYONNAISE, thinned with milk.

Combine all and mix thoroughly. Chill. Serve in bowl lined with lettuce leaves.

Turkey Waldorf Salad

A great way to serve Washington's abundant apples and tasty turkey for your Christmas luncheon.

3 RED DELICIOUS APPLES, cored, cut into 1/2 in. chunks
3 GRANNY SMITH APPLES, cored, cut into 1/2 in. chunks
2 Tbsp. LEMON JUICE
4 stalks CELERY, diced
3/4 cup PITTED DATES, chopped
3 cups ROAST TURKEY, cubed
1/2 cup MAYONNAISE
1/2 cup WHIPPING CREAM, whipped
3/4 cup WALNUTS, coarsely chopped
SALT, FRESHLY GROUND PEPPER to taste

Toss apple chunks with lemon juice in mixing bowl. Mix in celery, dates and turkey. In separate small bowl, gently fold together mayonnaise and whipped cream. Blend into salad ingredients until well combined. Fold in walnuts and season to taste. Cover; refrigerate until serving.

Laverne's Favorite Salad

"This was our family's favorite gelatin salad. My wife, Laverne, made this for our boys at Christmastime."—Bill Peterson, Everett

1 pkg. (6 oz.) LIME GELATIN
4 cups BOILING WATER
4 cups MINI MARSHMALLOWS
1 can (20 oz.) CRUSHED PINEAPPLE, drained
2 Tbsp. LEMON JUICE
1 cup NUTS, chopped
1 pkg. (8 oz.) CREAM CHEESE, softened
2 cups WHIPPING CREAM

Dissolve gelatin in water, add marshmallows to hot liquid. Stir until dissolved. Add pineapple, lemon juice, nuts and cream cheese. Chill till slightly firm; whip cream and stir into gelatin mixture. Chill until set in a 9 x 13 pan.

Frosty Christmas Grapes

1/2 cup SUGAR
2 env. UNFLAVORED GELATIN
10 sm. GRAPE CLUSTERS

Combine sugar and gelatin; mix well. Dip grape clusters in water; shake off excess water. Sprinkle sugar mixture through a sieve over wet grapes. Place on waxed paper about 45 minutes until dry. Arrange in your favorite Christmas dish.

Chapter Three

Deck the Halls

There may be chestnuts roasting on the open fire, but if there aren't decorations, it still may not seem like Christmas. In the past, a home that observed the traditional Christmas would probably have been decked out with holly, ivy and mistletoe long before Christmas Eve.

While those items are still used today, we have added much more. So, let's *deck the halls,* and the house! Let's start with the banisters, and wrap them with candy-striped ribbon or pine boughs, or maybe balls, candy or tiny lights. A lighted garland is very nice for that special touch.

Try using colored cellophane taped to your window panes. The children will love making the windows look like stained glass. Frame a window with ribbon and add a bow to create a big 'package'.

Decorating with wreaths can be fun for the whole family. Craft shops have all kinds of materials for creating your own special motif. Bend a metal coathanger (you may need pliers) to form a circle for the base of your wreath. Now add greenery and bows, tiny Christmas ornaments, or any of the many Christmas trimmings available.

As in *The Night Before Christmas,* the stockings are hung with loving care around the fireplace. If you have no fireplace, hang them at the windowsill!

Christmas cards begin arriving around the first of December. If you display them, it helps make the home more festive and colorful. Tie bows of red velvet and attach a length of ribbon to each. Hang them from a door or on a wall. Use straight pins to attach your cards to the ribbons.

Another merry way you could present the season is by folding green or red napkins around the silverware settings and placing them in a small baskets decorated with ribbons.

Centerpieces of red carnations, a sprig of pine, or a wreath of gourds around a bowl of red Washington apples create a festive atmosphere.

For a truly old-fashioned Christmas, string popcorn and cranberries for your tree and let the children decorate their own Christmas cooky ornaments.

Let the warmth and joy of the Christmas season be the most impartant part of your celebrations.

We Three Kings of Orient Are . . .

Images of the three kings (Magi) and their gifts are unvarying elements in Nativity scenes. The three kings were Melchior, king of Arabia and the bearer of gold; Balthazar, king of Ethiopia and the bearer of frankincense; and Caspar, king of Tarsus, who brought myrrh.

Soups

Oyster Stew

CLARIFIED BUTTER
1/2 tsp. GARLIC
1/2 tsp. SHALLOTS
1/2 tsp. CAJUN SPICE
1/2 tsp. CHICKEN BASE
6 to 8 sm. to med. OYSTERS
1/2 oz. BRANDY
HEAVY CREAM
GREEN ONIONS, chopped

In a small sauté pan, place enough butter to cover bottom. Add garlic, shallots, spice and chicken base. Add oysters, flame with brandy. Add heavy cream, heat and top with green onions.

Sour Cream Potato Soup

3 cups POTATOES, diced
1/2 cup CELERY, diced
1/2 cup ONIONS, diced
1 1/2 cups WATER
2 CHICKEN BOUILLON CUBES
SALT, to taste
2 cups MILK, divided
1 cup SOUR CREAM
2 Tbsp. FLOUR
2 Tbsp. CHIVES
GRATED CHEESE, for garnish

Combine potatoes, celery, onions, water, bouillon and salt. Cover and cook until tender. Gradually add one cup of milk. In a small bowl, combine sour cream, flour, chives and remaining milk; gradually stir into cooked potatoes. Cook over low heat until thick. Serve with grated cheese.

Hearty Split Pea Soup

"Every family has its own special way of preparing this soup. We hope your family will think this is the very best for the holidays."—Joanie Anderson, Spokane

1 1/2 lb. HAM HOCKS	**1 tsp. SALT**
1 lb. DRIED SPLIT PEAS	**4 whole PEPPERCORNS**
1 1/4 cups CARROTS, chopped	**4 whole ALLSPICE**
1/2 cup ONIONS, sliced	**1 BAY LEAF**
8 cups WATER	

Combine ham hocks, peas, carrots, onions, water and salt in Dutch oven. Cover and bring to a boil. Meanwhile, tie spices in small piece of cheese cloth; add to pea mixture. Reduce heat and simmer 45 minutes, or until peas are tender. Discard spice bag. Remove ham hocks from soup and remove meat from bones. Cut ham into chunks and return to soup.

Cream Soup Base

2 cups NONFAT DRY MILK
3/4 cup CORN STARCH
1/4 cup INSTANT CHICKEN BOUILLON
2 Tbsp. ONION FLAKES
1 tsp. BASIL
1 tsp. THYME
1/2 tsp. PEPPER

In container, with tight fitting lid, combine all ingredients. Shake to mix thoroughly before each use. To make the equivalent of one can of soup, in saucepan, combine 1/3 cup of dry mixture and 1 1/4 cups of cold water. Cook until thick. Be creative; add cheese, cooked meat or vegetables.

"Zalig Kerstfeest" . . . *Merry Christmas in Dutch*

Clam Chowder

1 lb. BACON, cut in 1/8 in. pieces
3 stalks CELERY, sliced thin
1 lg. ONION, sliced thin
3 med. POTATOES, with skins
1 box (6 oz.) DRY HASH BROWNS
2 cans CHOPPED CLAMS, with juice
1 can (10 oz.) WHOLE BABY CLAMS, with juice
PARSLEY, CHIVES and SEASONINGS, to taste
2 cans EVAPORATED MILK

Pan fry bacon until crisp; reserve fat and set aside. In reserved fat, sauté celery and onions until transparent. Boil sliced or large cubed potatoes until semi-tender, with just enough water to cover. Reconstitute hash browns. Combine onions, celery, bacon, clams, spices and milk with potatoes. Add just enough hash browns to thicken. Serve in warm bowls with pat of butter; add cream on top if desired.

Shrimp & Corn Chowder

1/4 cup GREEN PEPPER, diced
1 Tbsp. MARGARINE
3 oz. CREAM CHEESE
2 cans CREAM OF POTATO SOUP
1 1/2 soup cans MILK
2 cans SHRIMP
1 can WHOLE KERNEL CORN, undrained

Sauté pepper in margarine; cook until tender. Add cream cheese, stir until blended. Add remaining ingredients; bring to boil. Reduce heat, cover and simmer 10 minutes.

Moushella

"Being of German heritage, my uncle makes this every year. It requires a bit of time, but is quite worth the effort. It's referred to as a German version of Won Ton soup."—Marilyn Tatham, Snohomish

Noodle Dough (Step One):
3 EGGS
3 cups FLOUR
1 tsp. SALT

Meatball Mix (Step Two):
1 1/2 lbs. HAMBURGER
1/2 lb. PORK SAUSAGE, unseasoned
1 1/2 tsp. SALT
3/4 tsp. PEPPER
1/4 tsp. ALLSPICE
1/8 tsp. THYME
dash CLOVES
dash MACE
dash SAVORY
2 cloves GARLIC, crushed

Step Three:
2 lg. cans BEEF BROTH
2 lg. ONIONS, diced
1 clove GARLIC, crushed
4 qts. WATER, approx.

Step One: Mix noodle ingredients, kneading with hands, to make very firm dough. You may need to add flour or a little water. Cut dough into quarters; roll until very thin. Cut into 4 x 4 inch squares; set aside until meatballs are made. Step Two: Combine all meatball ingredients; form into small balls. Wrap in noodle squares, making triangles. Seal edges of dough with water, or a bit of egg white. Step Three: In large kettle, combine ingredients; bring to boil. Drop in noodle meat squares, one at a time. They will rise to the top. Boil gently about 20 minutes.

Christmas Corn Chowder

"This is hearty enough to be a one pot meal, because of the bacon, sausage and potatoes."—Rebecca Smith, Wenatchee

1/2 lb. SLICED BACON
1 cup CELERY, chopped
1/2 cup ONION, chopped
2 cups POTATOES, peeled, diced
1 cup WATER
2 cups FROZEN CORN
1 can (14 1/2 oz.) CREAM STYLE CORN
1 can (12 oz.) EVAPORATED MILK
6 oz. SMOKED SAUSAGE, cut into 1/4 in. slices
1 tsp. DILL WEED

In a large saucepan, cook bacon until crisp. Remove to paper towel, crumble and set aside. Reserve 2 Tbsp. of bacon drippings; sauté celery and onions in drippings until lightly browned. Add potatoes and water. Cover and cook over medium heat 10 minutes. Stir in corns, milk, sausage, dill and bacon. Cook until potatoes are tender, about 30 minutes.

Christmas Eve Oyster Stew

2 to 3 jars SMALL OYSTERS   **1 qt. MILK**
1 cube MARGARINE   **BUTTER**
SEASONING SALT   **PARSLEY for garnish**

Drain oysters. In hot fry pan, sauté oysters in margarine with seasonings until edges are curly and oysters are fried firm. Add milk, heat until milk is hot, but not scalded. Taste; adjust seasonings. Serve in bowl with pat of butter. Garnish; serve with hot french bread or sourdough rolls. Do not be stingy with butter, seasonings or oysters.

Tex-Mex Tortilla Soup

2 lbs. CHICKEN BREASTS, skinned, boned
2 cups WATER
1 can (14 1/2 oz.) BEEF BROTH
1 can (14 1/2 oz.) CHICKEN BROTH
1 can (14 1/2 oz.) TOMATOES, cut up, undrained
1/2 cup ONION, chopped
1/4 cup GREEN PEPPER, chopped
1 (8 3/4 oz. can) WHOLE KERNEL CORN, drained
1 tsp. CHILI POWDER
1/2 tsp. CUMIN
1/8 tsp. PEPPER
TORTILLA CHIPS, coarsely crushed, about 3 cups
1 cup MONTEREY JACK CHEESE, grated
1 AVOCADO, cut into chunks

Cut chicken into 1 inch cubes, set aside. In a large saucepan, combine water, broths, tomatoes, onion and green pepper; bring to boiling. Add chicken; reduce heat. Cover, simmer for 10 minutes. Add corn, and spices. Simmer, covered, for 10 minutes more. Place chips in serving bowls. Ladle soup over chips; sprinkle with cheese and avocado.

Las Posadas . . .

The Spanish Christmas tradition of Las Posadas is a reenactment of the search of Joseph and Mary for lodging in Bethlehem. Nine days before Christmas, villagers taking the part of pilgrims travel from home to home asking for shelter. When they are admitted the following prayer is spoken:

O God, who in coming to save us,
did not disdain a humble stable,
grant that we may never close our
hearts when thou art knocking
so that we may be made worthy to be
received into thy sight when our hour
comes.

Chapter Four

Silent Night, Holy Night

On the day before Christmas Eve in 1818 Joseph Mohr, the parish priest of the little church in Arnsdorf, Austria, wrote the words to *Silent Night*. He took them to the church's organist, Franz Gruber, who like many organists at that time was an accomplished music writer. One of our most reverent carols resulted from their combined efforts.

Many carols originated in Europe. The German words *O Tannenbaum* were set to music in what is one of the oldest tunes in existence. This traditional German carol became the song we Washingtonians love as, *O Christmas Tree*.

Christmas music has become a tradition of the season here in Washington. Many churches now invite the public to their 'Living Christmas Trees', as choirs proudly sing favorite carols, such as *Away in a Manger*, a simple hymn loved by children everywhere.

One of the early traditional Christmas carols was *Jolly Old St. Nicholas* which later evolved into many more modern tunes, such as *I Saw Mommy Kissing Santa Claus*.

When St. Nick arrived in America, he was a chubby, robust Santa Claus, a relative of the Dutch *Sinter Klauss*. Children of the Dutch farming community of Lynden, Washington, still follow the ageless customs of their fore-fathers in their community's Christmas celebrations.

Years ago, the little Dutch children had a custom of filling a wooden shoe with straw, and placing it on their windowsill for St. Nick's white horse. In the morning, they found the straw had been replaced with sweets and gifts.

The Dutch have relied on herring and other fish for centuries, because of their proximity to the sea. However, they also have a great fondness for soup, usually preferring that it be hearty and full bodied. According to Dutch legend, pea soup must be so thick that the spoon will remain upright. Try the delicious pea soup recipe on page 34.

The Twelve Days of Christmas

On the first day of Christmas my true love gave to me . . .

A partridge in a pear tree...

Two turtle doves...

Three French hens...

Four calling birds...

Five gold rings...

Six geese a' laying...

Seven swans a' swimming...

Eight maids a' milking...

Nine ladies dancing...

Ten lords a' leaping...

Eleven pipers piping...

Twelve drummers drumming...

Side Dishes

Festive Sweet Potatoes

"I fix this for Christmas dinner, and call it 'Sweet Potato Recipe for Sweet Potato Haters'. I get so many requests for this recipe that I have to keep extra copies on hand."—Phyllis Morgan, **Fulton House Bed & Breakfast**, Mt. Vernon

3 cups SWEET POTATOES, cooked, mashed
1/2 cup SUGAR
1/4 cup MILK
1/3 cup MARGARINE, melted
1 tsp. VANILLA EXTRACT
2 EGGS, beaten
1 cup FLAKED COCONUT
1 cup BROWN SUGAR, firmly packed
1/3 cup FLOUR
1/3 cup MARGARINE, melted
1 cup PECANS

Combine first six ingredients, mixing well. Spoon into lightly greased 8 inch square baking dish. Combine remaining ingredients, sprinkle over top of sweet potatoes. Bake at 375 degrees, about 25 minutes or until golden brown.

Super Quick & Easy Dressing

1 med. ONION, chopped
CELERY, to taste, chopped
3 Tbsp. MARGARINE
2 pkgs. SEASONED DRESSING MIX
2 cans CHICKEN RICE SOUP

Saute onion and celery in margarine until partially tender. Combine with dressing mix and soup, mixing well. Bake in 350 degree oven about 30 minutes, until heated through.

Christmas Relish

"This is a scrumptious side dish! It also makes a fabulous dessert torte. It is as pleasing to the eye as it is to the palate."—**Mio Amore Pensione,** *Trout Lake*

2 APPLES, peeled, cored and cut in 1/2 in. pieces
1 pkg. fresh CRANBERRIES
1 1/4 cups SUGAR
1 cup RAISINS
1/2 cup ORANGE JUICE
1 tsp. CINNAMON
1 Tbsp. GRAND MARNIER or ORANGE LIQUEUR
2 cans MANDARIN ORANGES, drained

Combine apples, cranberries, sugar, raisins, orange juice and cinnamon in heavy, large saucepan. Stir over medium heat until mixture comes to a boil. Reduce heat to medium low, simmer about 20 minutes until mixture thickens and leaves path on bottom of pan when spoon is drawn across, stirring occasionally. Remove from heat, mix in grand marnier and orange segments. Transfer to bowl, let cool. Press plastic wrap directly on surface, and refrigerate until well chilled. Can be prepared a day ahead.

Caramelized Onions

3 Tbsp. BUTTER
3 Tbsp. BROWN SUGAR
1/2 cup CHICKEN BROTH
1 (16 oz. pkg.) FROZEN SMALL WHOLE ONIONS

Melt butter in large skillet over medium high heat; add brown sugar and broth and mix well. Bring to boil; add onions and cook uncovered 15 to 20 minutes, stirring frequently. Onions should be glazed and most of the liquid evaporated.

Potato Filling

"Mashed potatoes were always served with an unstuffed roasted turkey at my Pennsylvania Dutch Grandmother's Christmas dinner."—Evelyn Tuller, **Moon & Sixpence**, Friday Harbor

1/2 cup CELERY, chopped
1 ONION, chopped
1/2 cup BUTTER, melted
4 cups SOFT BREAD CUBES
1/2 cup BOILING WATER
2 cups MILK
SALT & PEPPER, to taste
2 cups MASHED POTATOES

Sauté celery and onions in butter until tender; add bread and water. Mix well. Add remaining ingredients. Finished product should be very moist; add more milk, if necessary. Turn into greased casserole dish; bake at 350 degrees for 45 minutes.

 ## Song for St. Nicholas' Day

(December 6th)

In Dutch and in English

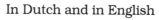

Sint Nikolaas Kapoentje,	*Santa Claus, Kapoentje,*
Gooi wat in myn schoentje.	*Throw something in my shoes.*
Gooi wat in myn laarsje,	*Throw something in my boots,*
Dank je Sint Nikolaasje.	*Thank you, Santa Claus*

Oyster Stuffing

"This recipe for oyster stuffing has always been a family favorite for those winter Holiday turkey dinners. Mother always put half in the turkey cavity, and the balance around the turkey."—Jean Sherman, Everett

3 pts. OYSTERS, chopped, reserve liquid
3/4 cup MARGARINE
1 1/2 cups CELERY, chopped
1 1/2 cups ONIONS, chopped
12 cups DRY BREAD CUBES
3 Tbsp. PARSLEY, chopped
3 tsp. SALT
1/2 tsp. POULTRY SEASONING
1/4 tsp. BLACK PEPPER

Drain oysters. Melt margarine in skillet, add celery and onions, cooking until tender but not brown. Combine oysters with celery, onion, bread cubes, parsley and spices; mix well. Moisten stuffing with oyster liquid, if necessary. Makes enough for a 10 to 15 lb. turkey. Stuffing may be baked in lightly greased casserole at 325 degrees for 45 minutes to an hour or until heated through.

Baked Cranberry Sauce

A delicious turkey or ham accompaniment.

1 lb. CRANBERRIES
1 (12 oz. jar) ORANGE MARMALADE
3/4 cup SUGAR
1/4 cup WATER
1 cup PECANS, toasted, chopped

Preheat oven to 350 degrees; combine all ingredients, except nuts, in a 9 x 13 glass baking dish. Bake uncovered, 45 minutes. Stir in pecans. Serve warm or chilled. Cover and refrigerate up to a week.

Holiday Creamed Onions

"This is always a big hit at our Christmas dinners."—Opal Watson, Vancouver

1 pkg. (16 oz.) SMALL WHOLE ONIONS
2 Tbsp. MARGARINE
2 Tbsp. FLOUR
1/8 tsp. SALT
1/8 tsp. WHITE PEPPER
1 cup CHICKEN BROTH
2/3 cup MILK
1/4 cup SHARP CHEDDAR CHEESE, grated

Cook onions according to directions, drain and set aside. In large skillet over medium heat, melt margarine. Add flour, salt and pepper. Cook, stirring constantly until mixture is smooth and bubbly. Gradually add chicken broth and milk. Cook until mixture boils and thickens, stirring constantly. Stir in cheese and onions; cook additional 5 minutes or until thoroughly heated, stir occasionally.

Asparagus with Parmesan

1 cup CHICKEN BROTH
1 bunch ASPARAGUS, trimmed or a large
    package (16 oz.), frozen
Fresh LEMON JUICE to taste
2 - 3 Tbsp. PARMESAN CHEESE, freshly grated

Bring chicken broth to a boil in a frying pan. Add asparagus, cover and simmer about 7 minutes, or until desired doneness. Drain, remove from pan and add lemon juice and Parmesan cheese.

Cornbread Stuffing

2 cups ONION, chopped
1 cup CELERY, chopped
1/4 cup MARGARINE
1 (13 3/4 oz. can) CHICKEN BROTH
1 (17 oz. can) WHOLE KERNEL CORN, drained
1 (7 oz. can) DICED GREEN CHILES
3 Tbsp. PARSLEY, chopped
1/2 tsp. POULTRY SEASONING
1/2 tsp. SALT
PEPPER, to taste
1/4 tsp. OREGANO
6 cups CRUMBLED CORNBREAD or DRY CORNBREAD
    STUFFING MIX
1/2 cup PECANS, chopped

Heat oven to 350 degrees. In large Dutch oven, sauté onion and celery in margarine until tender. Stir in remaining ingredients except cornbread and pecans, mixing well. Add cornbread and pecans, tossing gently until moistened evenly. Spoon into casserole dish; cover and bake 30 minutes or until heated through.

Health, Peace, and
sweet content
be yours.
Shakespeare

Chanterelle Pie

"This is best with fresh chanterelles. They grow abundantly in the old growth forests in northwestern Washington. Fun to pick, and then home to enjoy the bounty. This is one of my favorites." — Juanita Warber, **Ocean Crest Resort,** Moclips

1 pkg. (8 oz.) CREAM CHEESE
1/2 cup BUTTER, softened
1 1/2 cups FLOUR
3 lbs. CHANTERELLE
    MUSHROOMS, sliced
2 Tbsp. BUTTER
1 med. ONION, sliced
1 tsp. SALT
1/2 tsp. PEPPER
1 tsp. PARSLEY OR SAGE
2 Tbsp. LEMON JUICE
1 cup SOUR CREAM

Combine first 3 ingredients to make a soft crust; chill for 15 minutes. Sauté mushrooms in butter, add onions and cook until tender. Sprinkle with seasonings and lemon juice. Remove from heat, add sour cream. Fill pie shell and cover with top crust. Bake at 375 degrees for 40 minutes.

Scalloped Oysters

*"A family favorite. My son insists on these
every holiday season.."—Opal Watson, Vancouver*

1 1/2 cups CRACKER CRUMBS
1/2 cup MARGARINE, melted
1 pt. OYSTERS, drained, reserve liquid
1/2 tsp. SALT
1/4 tsp. PEPPER
HALF AND HALF

Combine crumbs with margarine, spread 1/3 of crumbs on bottom of greased 10 x 6 casserole. Arrange oysters on top; Sprinkle with salt and pepper. To the oyster liquid, add enough half and half to measure 2/3 cup. Pour over oysters; top with remaining crumbs. Bake, uncovered, at 400 degrees until golden brown, about 20 to 30 minutes.

Christmas Zucchini & Tomatoes

2 ZUCCHINI, sliced or small package (10-12 oz.) frozen
1 -2 cloves GARLIC, minced
2 Tbsp. OLIVE OIL
1 can (14 1/2 oz.) TOMATOES, Italian style
1/4 tsp. BASIL LEAVES
1/4 tsp. OREGANO LEAVES
1/4 tsp. PEPPER

Sauté the zucchini and garlic in the olive oil for about 5 minutes. Add the tomatoes and roughly half of the juice and the seasonings. Gently simmer until zucchini is done to taste.

Chapter Five

Bring on the Turkey!

We know that turkey is the most popular main course for holiday dinners. Each family has their own preference for stuffing and roasting the bird. On page 59 we have included a favorite *Roast Turkey* recipe and a chart for roasting times.

For those who want a "different taste" for their Christmas dinner see the recipes for *Roast Leg of Lamb* (page 59) and *Perfect Prime Rib* (page 61). A Scandinavian-style smorgasbord of *Swedish Meatballs* (page 14), *Lutfisk* (page 56), *Fish Balls* (page 56), cranberries, several salads, breads and rolls can be prepared in advance so that on Christmas day no one has to spend too much time in the kitchen.

Select accompaniments from our Side Dish section and don't forget to add *Christmas Dinner Rolls* (page 68).

After dinner, it's dessert time! For many families, it's traditional pumpkin pie, chiffon pumpkin pie, fruit cake, mince pie and pecan pie.....maybe with just a dash of ice cream! You'll find tempting recipes in the Dessert Section.

We've even thought of those turkey leftovers! See the recipes for *Turkey Noodle Casserole* & *Turkey Casserole Au Gratin* in this section on page 60.

Whatever your preference for Christmas dinner may be, we hope this book adds to your families' enjoyment of this joyous occasion.

Main Dishes

Cabbage with Polish Sausage

"Great with baked potatoes, rye bread, apple salad and dessert. The 'old country' cooks preferred cooking their cabbage for one hour."—Betsy Mastalski, Anacortes

1 cup ONION, chopped
2 Tbsp. BUTTER
2 Tbsp. FLOUR
1 cup WATER
1/4 cup WHITE VINEGAR
3/4 tsp. SALT

1/2 tsp. SUGAR
1/4 tsp. PEPPER
3 qts. CABBAGE, shredded
6 POLISH SAUSAGES,
    cut in 1 in. slices

Sauté onion in butter until soft and lightly colored. Blend in flour, add water and vinegar. Cook, stirring constantly until mixture boils. Blend in salt, sugar and pepper; stir in cabbage and sausage. Cover and simmer about 20 minutes or until cabbage in tender. Stir occasionally.

Glazed Turkey Meatballs

1 lb. GROUND TURKEY
1/2 cup TART APPLES, shredded
3/4 tsp. SALT
1/8 tsp. GARLIC POWDER
2 tsp. COOKING OIL
1/2 cup APPLE JELLY
2 Tbsp. SPICY BROWN MUSTARD

In a medium bowl, combine turkey, apple, salt and garlic powder. Shape into 16 meatballs; heat oil in large skillet over medium heat. Add meatballs, cook and turn until brown (about 8 minutes). In small bowl, stir together jelly and mustard. Spoon over meatballs; simmer additional 8 to 10 minutes, or until glazed. Turn meatballs several times. Sauce will thicken as it cools.

In Polish say "Wesolych Swiat" for Merry Christmas.

Chile Cheese Bake

"My family loves this dish, which can be made the day before. It cooks while we open presents at Grandma's house."—**Margie's Inn on the Bay**, *Sequim*

6 slices BREAD, trimmed, buttered one side
2 cups CHEDDAR CHEESE, grated
2 cups MONTEREY JACK CHEESE, grated
1/2 can GREEN CHILES, chopped
6 EGGS
2 cups MILK
2 tsp. PAPRIKA
1 tsp. SALT
1/2 tsp. OREGANO
1/2 tsp. PEPPER
1/4 tsp. GARLIC POWDER
1/4 tsp. DRY MUSTARD

Place bread buttered side down in a 9 x 13 dish. Combine cheeses and sprinkle on bread. Sprinkle chiles on cheese; beat eggs, add milk and seasonings. Pour over cheese; cover with plastic or foil. Keep in refrigerator at least four hours, overnight is best. Bake at 325 degrees for 55 minutes.

Poinsettias

The poinsettia is considered "the flower of Christmas Eve." Poinsettias (a native plant of Mexico) were named after Dr. Joel Poinsett, the first foreign minister from the United States to Mexico.

Medallions of Pork with Spiced Applesauce

8 to 12 BONELESS TRIMMED PORK CHOPS
1/4 cup SOY SAUCE
2 Tbsp. DIJON MUSTARD
1/2 cup SHERRY
2 lg. GARLIC CLOVES, minced
2 Tbsp. GINGER, fresh scraped or,
    2 Tbsp. GROUND GINGER
1/2 tsp. THYME
1/2 tsp. PEPPER

Glaze:
   2 Tbsp. SHERRY
   3 Tbsp. LEMON JUICE
   2 Tbsp. SOY SAUCE
   1 (10 oz. jar) MINT JELLY

Spiced Applesauce:
   2 cups APPLESAUCE, unsweetened
   2 Tbsp. LEMON JUICE
   3 Tbsp. HORSERADISH SAUCE

Marinate pork chops in above ingredients for at least 2 hours, turning twice. Drain chops; barbecue or broil until done. (Depends of thickness of chops and heat of the fire.) Cook until chops loose pinkness; baste while cooking with marinade. Just before serving, boil the remaining marinade down to 2 Tbsp. and add glaze ingredients. Glaze chops just before serving. Serve applesauce with chops. This savory sauce is equally good with lamb or beef dishes.

Chicken or Turkey Tetrazzini

This recipe is wonderful for using up your leftover Christmas turkey."—*Betsy Mastalski, Anacortes*

1 can CREAM OF MUSHROOM SOUP
1 can BEEF CONSOMMÉ
1/2 tsp. GARLIC POWDER
1/4 tsp. PEPPER
1 can MUSHROOMS, with liquid
2 Tbsp. FLOUR
1/2 cup MILK
1/2 lb. SPAGHETTI, cooked, drained
1/8 cup PARSLEY, chopped
3 to 4 cups COOKED CHICKEN OR TURKEY
1/2 cup RITZ® CRACKERS, crushed
2 slices BACON, crisp, crumbled

In a saucepan, combine soups and bring to boil, stirring constantly. Mix in garlic powder, pepper, and mushrooms; reduce heat and let sauce simmer. Prepare thickening using flour mixed with milk, add to simmering sauce and bring to boil stirring until smooth. Remove from heat and set aside. Line bottom of 9 x 13 dish with half the cooked spaghetti, sprinkle half the parsley and half the meat on top. Ladle half of the prepared sauce on top; make another layer repeating this step. Sprinkle crackers and bacon on last, cover and bake at 425 degrees for 45 minutes. Remove cover for last 10 to 15 minutes so crackers can brown.

"Bono Natale"
Merry Christmas
in Italian

Lutfisk

Lutfisk is the time-honored fish dish served in Scandinavia as the main dish for Christmas Eve dinner or supper. Boiled potatoes with white sauce are always served with lutfisk when it is the main fish course. A smorgasbord served during the Christmas holidays should always include lutfisk.

DRIED CODFISH, prepared according to package directions resulting in 4 lbs. prepared fish
10-12 WHOLE CLOVES, crushed to fine pieces

Place in kettle of boiling, salted water and boil for 20 to 30 minutes or until soft. Drain in colander and separate into pieces. Remove any pieces of skin or bones. Sprinkle with crushed cloves. Serve hot, with both white sauce and melted butter, giving guests their choice.

Scandinavian Fish Balls

2 1/2 lbs. fresh WHITE FISH
**   such as halibut, cod, etc.**
4 medium POTATOES, boiled
1 Tbsp. BUTTER, softened

1 small ONION, grated
1 tsp. SALT
1 tsp. NUTMEG
2 cups MILK

In batches, run fish through food processor until finely chopped. Also process boiled potatoes until just mashed. Blend with the fish mixture. Stir in butter, onion, salt, nutmeg and milk. Shape into small balls (add more milk if necessary, to make balls easier to handle). Boil in **Fish Broth** for about 10 minutes. Serve hot.

Fish Broth

FISH HEAD and BONES
1 quart WATER
1 tsp. SALT

Boil together for about 20 minutes. Strain, and return to kettle.

Authentic Swedish Meatballs

"Many years ago a Swedish friend, Grethel Osbjornson, gave me this recipe. It is a traditional Swedish Christmas Eve dinner, accompanied with baked halibut, fruit salad and Christmas desserts."—Annette Wilkins, Bellingham

2 slices BREAD
1/2 cup HEAVY CREAM
1/2 cup ONION, minced, browned in butter
1 lb. GROUND BEEF
1/2 lb. GROUND PORK or UNSEASONED SAUSAGE
1/4 lb. GROUND VEAL
4 EGG YOLKS
2 WHOLE EGGS
1/4 cup BUTTER
1 tsp. SALT
GROUND PEPPER

Brown Sauce:
  1 Tbsp. BUTTER
  1 Tbsp. FLOUR
  1 cup WATER
  1 BOUILLION CUBE
  1 cup HEAVY CREAM

Remove crust from bread; discard. Crumble remaining bread into cream; soak 10 minutes. Grind onions and meats in meat grinder. Combine eggs with bread, salt and pepper. Add to meat; mix well. Shape into balls; sauté a few at a time in butter. After each pan of sautéed meatballs make a brown sauce. Make roux from pan residue; adding butter, flour and water with bouillion. Add to pan and make gravy; set aside. Use heavy cream in place of water every other pan full. Place meatballs in large pan and simmer. Serve the meatballs with a ladle of brown sauce on top.

In Swedish, "Glad Jul" means Merry Christmas!

Chicken & Herb Dumplings

Dumplings are a staple of German cooks. Some are even poached in a fruit sauce and served for Christmas dessert!

2 (3 lb.ea.) CHICKENS, cut up
4 cups WATER
1 1/2 cups CELERY, chopped
1 1/2 cups CARROTS, chopped
1 1/2 cups ONIONS, chopped
1 Tbsp. SALT
1 1/2 tsp. DRIED THYME, crushed
1/8 tsp. PEPPER
1 cup COLD WATER
1/2 cup FLOUR
1 (10 oz. pkg.) FROZEN PEAS
1 (4 oz. can) MUSHROOMS STEMS & PIECES, undrained
2 Tbsp. PARSLEY, snipped

Herb Dumplings:

1 1/2 cups FLOUR
1 Tbsp. BAKING POWDER
3/4 tsp. SALT
1/4 tsp. DRIED THYME,
  crushed

3/4 cup SOUR CREAM
3/4 cup MILK
2 Tbsp. COOKING OIL

In Dutch oven or kettle, place chicken pieces. Add 4 cups water, celery, carrots, onions, salt, thyme and pepper. Bring to a boil. Reduce heat, cover and simmer 35 to 45 minutes until chicken is nearly tender. Skim off fat. Blend one cup water and flour, stir into chicken mixture. Stir in peas and mushrooms. Cook, stirring gently until thickened and bubbly.

Dumplings: In a medium bowl, thoroughly stir together the dry ingredients and spices. In another bowl, combine sour cream, milk, and oil. Add sour cream mixture all at once to dry ingredients in mixing bowl. Stir just till all dry ingredients are thoroughly moistened. Drop dumpling dough from tablespoon to make 8 mounds atop bubbling stew. Reduce heat, cover and simmer 15 minutes. **Do not lift cover.** Sprinkle with parsley.

Roast Leg of Lamb

"Serve whole, to be cut at the table, or slice in the kitchen and serve with potatoes, peas and carrots."—*Grace Ingvarsson, Everett*

1 LEG OF LAMB
SALT, PEPPER

Wipe the lamb with a cloth, dampened in warm water. Rub spices well into meat. Grease bottom of oven pan; place a few dots of margarine on top of roast. Bake in 450 degree oven for 15 to 20 minutes; reduce heat to 350 degrees. Pour small amount of hot water into pan. Cook for about 15 minutes per pound, basting occasionally with pan juices. May need to add water during baking. If juices are too fatty, skim first before making gravy.

Roast Turkey

Place prepared turkey in open roasting pan. Rub bird lightly on exposed surfaces with vegetable shortening. Rub inside cavities with salt. Place in preheated oven, roast uncovered until golden brown. Remove from oven, baste with pan juices, place a tent of foil over bird and return to oven. Add water to the pan drippings, in order to have ample juices for gravy. Roast in a 325 degree oven according to table below:

6 to 8 lbs.	3 to 3 1/2 hours
8 to 12 lbs.	3 1/2 to 4 hours
12 to 16 lbs.	4 to 5 hours
16 to 20 lbs.	5 to 6 hours
20 to 24 lbs.	6 to 6 3/4 hours

Roasting time is approximate, since confirmation of turkey, accuracy of oven, and degree of thawness are all variable. It is advisable to thaw turkey in your refrigerator, allowing 2 to 3 days for smaller birds and 3 to 5 days for larger birds.

Turkey Noodle Casserole

2 Tbsp. BUTTER
1 cup MUSHROOMS, sliced
1 sm. ONION, chopped
1 can CREAM OF CHICKEN SOUP
1 can CREAM OF MUSHROOM SOUP
1 cup WATER
2 Tbsp. SHERRY or ORANGE JUICE
8 oz. SPAGHETTI, cooked, drained
1/4 cup PIMIENTOS, chopped
2 Tbsp. PARSLEY, chopped
1/2 cup PARMESAN CHEESE, divided
2 cups COOKED TURKEY, cubed

Over medium heat in a 2 qt. saucepan, heat butter and cook mushrooms and onions until tender. Stir in soups, water and sherry and heat through. Stir in spaghetti, pimientos, parsley and 1/4 cup of the parmesan cheese. Stir in turkey; pour spaghetti mixture into 2 qt. casserole. Top with remaining parmesan cheese; bake at 375 degrees for 30 minutes or until hot and bubbling.

Turkey Casserole Au Gratin

2 cups COOKED TURKEY, cubed
2 cups SEASONED CUBED STUFFING MIX
1 cup CHEDDAR CHEESE, grated, divided
1 cup CELERY, thinly sliced
1 (10 1/2 oz. can) TURKEY GRAVY
1/4 cup ONION, chopped
dash PEPPER

In a bowl, combine turkey, stuffing, 1/2 cup cheese, celery, gravy, onion and pepper. Spoon mixture into 10 x 6 baking dish; bake at 350 degrees for 35 minutes. Sprinkle with remaining cheese and bake 10 minutes more, or until cheese melts.

Perfect Prime Rib

An elegant change from the traditional Christmas turkey.

FOOD GRADE ROCK SALT
BEEF RIB ROAST
SEASONING SALT

PEPPER
PREPARED MUSTARD
HORSERADISH SAUCE

Cover bottom of roasting pan with rock salt; place roast, bone side down on bed of salt. For each 4 lbs. of meat, season with 1 Tbsp. seasoning salt and 1 tsp. of pepper. Cover completely with a heavy coating of mustard; roll in rock salt pressing firmly into meat. Cover roast completely with rock salt. Place in preheated 210 degree oven and bake 9 to 10 hours until meat thermometer registers 140 degrees. Remove from oven; let stand 30 minutes. When ready to serve, remove from salt, transfer to plate and carve. Serve with horseradish sauce.

Turkey & Stuffing Hot Dish

An excellent dish for a family get-together.

4 cups HERB SEASONED STUFFING MIX
1 cup MARGARINE, melted
1 can CREAM OF CELERY SOUP
1 can CREAM OF MUSHROOM SOUP
1 (12 oz. can) EVAPORATED MILK
2 Tbsp. ONION, grated
1 (10 oz. pkg.) FROZEN PEAS, thawed
4 cups COOKED TURKEY, cubed

In large bowl, combine stuffing mix and margarine. Mix well; spread half of mixture in 9 x 13 baking pan. In another large bowl, combine soups, milk and onion; mix well. Stir in peas and turkey; mix well and spread over stuffing layer. Cover with remaining stuffing mixture and bake at 350 degrees for 45 minutes.

Chapter Six

Christmas Cards . . .

Who created the first Christmas card? It may have been the Englishman Henry Cole, who later became Sir Henry, the first director of the Victoria and Albert Museum. He wrote in his diary in 1843, "Mr. (John) Horsley came and brought a design for a Christmas card." Sir Henry sent roughly drawn copies to his friends and family that year.

Having received many compliments about the cards, Sir Henry later lithographed 1,000 copies of the design to sell in his shop. It depicted a family full of good cheer surrounded by a rustic trellis. After he began selling his cards, it still took over ten years for the custom to catch on.

Today, Christmas cards come in a huge variety of sizes and shapes. Imagine Mr. Cole's expression if he could see one of our modern cards that include music, recorded messages and even the wonderful smells of pine boughs.

Brunches & Breads

Christmas Tea Ring

"My family says it wouldn't be Christmas without the Christmas Tea Ring. My children are all married, and have children of their own, but still wait for me to make this special bread. We always put a candle on the bread for Christ's birthday celebration. The grandchildren carry on the tradition by blowing out the candle."— Barbie Guay, **Albatross Bed & Breakfast,** Anacortes

2 pkgs. DRY YEAST
1/4 cup WARM WATER
1/2 cup SUGAR
1/4 cup SHORTENING
1 tsp. SALT
1 cup MILK, hot, scalded
2 EGGS, unbeaten
5 to 5 1/2 cups FLOUR, sifted
MELTED BUTTER

Pineapple Date Filling:
1 No. 2 can CRUSHED PINEAPPLE, well drained
3/4 cup SUGAR
1 Tbsp. CORNSTARCH
3/4 cup DATES, chopped
1/2 cup WALNUTS, chopped
1/2 cup BROWN SUGAR, firmly packed
2 tsp. CINNAMON

Glaze:
1 cup POWDERED SUGAR, sifted
2 Tbsp. CREAM
1/2 tsp. VANILLA
CHOPPED NUTS
MARASCHINO CHERRY HALVES

Soften yeast in warm water, set aside. Combine sugar, shortening, salt, and milk in large mixing bowl; cool to lukewarm. Stir in eggs and softened yeast; add flour gradually to form stiff dough. Knead on floured surface until smooth and satiny, 5 to 8 minutes. Place in greased bowl

(Continued on next page)

(Continued from previous page)

and cover. Let rise in warm place until doubled, about 1 1/ 2 hours. Prepare filling. Combine in saucepan; pineapple, sugar and cornstarch and cook over medium heat until thick. Add dates and nuts; cool. After dough has risen, divide in half, roll out one portion on floured surface to 20 x 12 inch rectangle. Brush with melted butter. Spread with half the filling to within one inch of one long side and to edge of other side. Combine brown sugar and cinnamon; sprinkle half over filling on dough. Roll as for jelly roll, starting with covered 20 inch edge. Shape into a ring on greased cookie sheet. With scissors, make cuts one inch apart through top of ring to one inch from bottom. Alternate cut slices, bringing one to the center and the next to the outside of the ring. Cover. Repeat process with remaining dough. Let rise in warm place until light, 45 to 60 minutes. Bake at 375 degrees for 20 to 25 minutes. While warm, frost with vanilla glaze. Blend powdered sugar with cream and vanilla. Beat until spreading consistency. Garnish with nuts and cherries.

Flat-Bread

"Spread with butter to serve, along with paté, cheese, smoked herring, or whatever you fancy."—Grace Ingvarsson, Everett

1 lb. RYE FLOUR
1 to 1 1/4 cups BOILING WATER

Combine flour and water, knead. Divide into parts big enough to make thin, round cakes about the size of a dessert plate. Bake on very hot cast-iron griddle, turning often. If preferred, may use rye flour with white flour.

Sour Cream Coffee Cake

"We serve this at our annual Christmas brunch."—Phyllis Morgan, **Fulton House Bed & Breakfast**, Mt. Vernon

Cinnamon Nut Topping:
- **1/2 cup NUTS, chopped**
- **1 tsp. CINNAMON**
- **2 Tbsp. SUGAR**

Coffee Cake:
- **2 1/4 cups FLOUR, sifted**
- **2 tsp. BAKING POWDER**
- **1/2 tsp. BAKING SODA**
- **1/2 tsp. SALT**
- **3/4 cup BUTTER, room temperature**
- **1 1/2 cups SUGAR**
- **2 EGGS**
- **1 tsp. VANILLA**
- **1 cup SOUR CREAM, room temperature**

Preheat oven to 350 degrees, butter and flour a 9 inch tube pan or a 9 x 13 x 2 baking dish. (If using glass dish, preheat oven to 325 degrees.) Set aside. Prepare cinnamon nut topping and set aside. To sifted flour, add baking powder, soda and salt and sift again. Cream butter with sugar, add eggs and vanilla beating until light and fluffy. Add flour mixture in 3 portions, alternating with sour cream, and beating well after each addition. Spread half of batter in pan, sprinkle with half of cinnamon nut topping. Spoon on remaining batter and sprinkle with remaining topping. If using tube pan bake 45 to 50 minutes. Bake oblong cake 40 minutes. Cake begins to pull away from sides of pan when done. Cool 20 minutes before removing from pan. Serve warm or cool.

Spicy Chocolate Muffins

"We are big chocoholics here, and this is one of our favorites."—
Barbara DeFreygas, **North Garden Inn Bed &**
Breakfast, Bellingham

1/2 cup SHORTENING	1/2 tsp. CLOVES
1 cup SUGAR	1 tsp. BAKING SODA
2 EGGS	1 tsp. CINNAMON
1 tsp. VANILLA	1/4 tsp. GINGER
1 1/2 cups FLOUR	3/4 cup CANNED PUMPKIN
1/2 tsp. SALT	1 cup CHOCOLATE CHIPS
1/2 tsp. NUTMEG	1/2 cup NUTS, chopped

Cream shortening and sugar; add eggs and vanilla. Sift dry ingredients and add to mixture alternately with pumpkin. When mixed, stir in chocolate chips and nuts. Fill greased muffin cups 3/4 full. Bake at 325 degrees for 30 minutes.

Cranberry Muffins

"Very good for breakfast with coffee, or just as a snack."—
Juanita Warber, **Ocean Crest Resort,** Moclips

1 cup CRANBERRIES	1 1/2 tsp. BAKING POWDER
1/2 cup NUTS, chopped	1 tsp. SALT
1 Tbsp. ORANGE RIND, grated	2 Tbsp. SHORTENING
2 cups FLOUR	3/4 cup ORANGE JUICE
1 cup SUGAR	1 EGG, well beaten

Blend ingredients all together and place in either muffin tin or bread loaf pan. Bake at 350 degrees for 20 minutes, for muffins, or one hour for bread.

Christmas Dinner Rolls

"These are a family favorite year-round, and replace 'store bought' bread easily. These rolls freeze well."—Juanita Warber, **Ocean Crest Resort,** Moclips

10 tsp. YEAST
1/2 cup WARM WATER
3 cups HOT WATER
1/2 cup SHORTENING
3 1/2 cups EVAPORATED MILK
3 cups SUGAR
17 cups FLOUR, divided
6 EGGS

Mix yeast with warm water; set aside. Heat water hot enough to melt the shortening. In a large mixing bowl, place water, shortening mixture, milk, sugar, and 6 cups of flour; mix well. Add eggs; mix well. Add 2 cups of flour; mix well. Add yeast mixture; mix well. Add remaining flour, one cup at a time. Knead for a few minutes, let rest for 10 minutes. Knead until smooth; place in large greased bowl. Let rise until doubled; punch down. Form into 100 palm size balls; let rise until double. Bake for 20 to 25 minutes at 350 degrees, or for 7 minutes in a convection oven.

Pomander Balls . . .

Decorative and fragrant pomander balls are easy to make.

Use a small nail to cover apples, oranges and lemons with holes. Press whole cloves into the holes. Place the fruit in a paper bag with powdered cinnamon and shake well. Let dry for about 2 weeks.

Tie with fancy ribbons and hang them on your tree or arrange them in a bowl to create an attractive table decoration. They also make excellent Christmas gifts or stocking stuffers.

Scottish Scones

"At the Inn, we sprinkle these with red sugar at Christmas." —
Marisa Williams, **Harbinger Inn Bed & Breakfast***, Olympia*

1 1/2 cups FLOUR
3/4 cup ROLLED OATS
1/4 cup BROWN SUGAR
2 tsp. BAKING POWDER
1/2 tsp. SALT
1 tsp. CINNAMON
1/2 cup BUTTER
1/2 cup MILK

Topping:
    1 Tbsp. BUTTER, melted
    1 Tbsp. SUGAR
    1 tsp. CINNAMON

Heat oven to 350 degrees; grease cookie sheet. Mix all
dry ingredients; cut in softened butter. Add milk and mix.
Knead six times; press out into 6 inch circle on cookie sheet.
Brush with melted butter; sprinkle with sugar and cinnamon. Cut into eight wedges; bake 20 to 25 minutes.

Old-Fashioned Eggs

There is no trick to the preparation of this favorite American
breakfast dish, other than choosing fresh farm eggs and good
quality whipping cream." —*David Campiche,* **Shelburne Country**
Inn, *Seaview*

12 FRESH FARM EGGS   **SALT to taste**
1/4 cup HEAVY CREAM   **4 Tbsp. CLARIFIED BUTTER**

With a whip, beat eggs until foamy. Stir in cream and
salt. Keeping mixture moist, sauté immediately in butter.
(An addition of finely chopped fresh dill or cilantro is a nice
alternative.) Scrambled eggs should be stirred constantly in
sauté pan, and in our opinion, cooked on the lean side.

Yule Kage

(Norwegian Christmas Bread)

"Always on the morn of the 24th, we have Yule Kage, sometimes accompanied with smoked salmon, pickled herring and cheese"—Barbara DeFreygas, **North Garden Inn Bed & Breakfast,** Bellingham

2 pkgs. DRY YEAST
1/2 cup LUKEWARM WATER
3 cups MILK, scalded
1/2 cup BUTTER
1 cup SUGAR
2 tsp. SALT
10 to 11 cups FLOUR, divided
2 EGGS, beaten
3 cups CANDIED FRUIT
1/2 tsp. GROUND CARDAMOM

Dissolve yeast in water; set aside. Pour scalded milk over butter; cool to lukewarm. Add yeast, sugar, salt and half the flour; beat. Add eggs one at a time, beating well. Add fruit, cardamom, and enough flour to make a soft dough. Knead, place in greased bowl and let rise until doubled. Knead and let rise again. Knead again. Divide into round loaves. Let rise again; bake at 375 degrees for 45 to 50 minutes. After baking, brush tops with butter. You may place in refrigerator to rise overnight, covered with plastic.

"Gledelig Jul"
Merry Christmas in Norwegian

Christmas Morning Toast

"Guests enjoy this scrumptious toast on Christmas morning. It is tasty and unusual, and fills you up until Christmas dinner." — *Edel Sokol,* **Ann Starrett Mansion,** *Port Townsend*

Filling:
 8 oz. CREAM CHEESE, softened
 1 oz. LIQUEUR, (Benedictine & Brandy)
 5 MANGOES, cut into 1/2 in. pieces

French Toast:
 2 loaves SWEET FRENCH BREAD
 4 EGGS
 1 cup HALF AND HALF
 1 1/2 tsp. VANILLA

Sauce:
 4 MANGOES, cut into 1/2 in. pieces
 2 oz. GUAVA NECTAR
 2 oz. LIQUEUR (Benedictine & Brandy)
 UNSALTED BUTTER OR VEGETABLE OIL

Chocolate Glaze:
 1 oz. SEMI SWEET CHOCOLATE
 1 Tbsp. HALF AND HALF
 1 tsp. LIQUEUR (Benedictine & Brandy)

Beat cream cheese until fluffy; stir in liqueur. Mix in mangoes. Cut off ends of French loaves; slice crossways in 2 inch pieces. Make a slice in center of each piece without cutting all the way through. Fill center with cream cheese filling. (The filled toast may be refrigerated or frozen until ready to cook and serve.) Beat together eggs, half and half and vanilla; melt butter in heavy skillet over medium heat. Dip filled bread pieces in egg mixture, shaking off excess. Place on pan or griddle sliced side down. Sauté till golden brown and flip, adding more butter and cooking until second side is golden brown. Transfer bread to cookie sheet; bake for 20 minutes in a 200 degree oven. While baking, pureé

(continued on next page)

(continued from previous page)

mangoes with guava nectar and liqueur in blender. Place in top of double boiler and heat. In microwave, melt chocolate; add half and half and liqueur. If needed, additional half and half may be added for drizzling consistency. To serve, spread 2 oz. of sauce on plate; place filled toast on sauce. Spoon an additional ounce of sauce over top and drizzle with glaze, making a zigzag design.

Pumpkin Pancakes

Prof. James Walker—Pullman

2 cups FLOUR
1 Tbsp. BROWN SUGAR, packed
1 Tbsp. BAKING POWDER
1 tsp. CINNAMON
1/2 tsp. GINGER
1/2 tsp. NUTMEG
1/2 tsp. SALT
2 EGG WHITES
1 1/2 cups SKIM MILK
1/2 cup PUMPKIN
VEGETABLE OIL

Topping:
  1/2 lb. BUTTER, room temperature
  1/2 cup POWDERED SUGAR
  1 tsp. CINNAMON

About 30 minutes before serving, mix first 7 ingredients in large bowl; set aside. In a small bowl, combine egg whites, lightly beaten, with milk, pumpkin and 2 Tbsp. of oil. Add to flour mixture, stirring just until flour is moistened. Prepare just as you would any pancake. Whip together topping ingredients until fluffy and serve.

Sausage Gravy

"This gravy is a specialty at my house. It makes a real stick-to-the-ribs dish that we always enjoy served over hot biscuits."—Lisa Walker, Bellingham

1 lb. BULK PORK SAUSAGE
6 Tbsp. FLOUR
1 qt. MILK
1/4 tsp. SALT
dash WORCESTERSHIRE SAUCE
dash HOT PEPPER SAUCE
1/2 tsp. POULTRY SEASONING, optional
1/2 GROUND NUTMEG, optional

Crumble sausage into large saucepan; cook until well browned over medium low heat. Drain, discarding all but 2 Tbsp. of drippings. Stir in flour, cook over medium heat about 6 minutes or until mixture bubbles and turns golden. Stir in milk; add seasonings and cook, stirring, until thickened.

Icelandic Fried Crullers

4 cups FLOUR
3 tsp. BAKING POWDER
1 tsp. SALT
2 tsp. CARDAMOM

1/2 cup MARGARINE
4 1/2 Tbsp. SUGAR
1 EGG
7 Tbsp. MILK

Mix together the dry ingredients and add the margarine, sugar, egg and milk. Work into a dough. Roll out to about 1/8 inch thick. Cut into strips about 3/4 inch wide and 3 inches long; in a slant wise direction, using a pastry wheel. Make a slit in center of each cruller; pull one end of strip through slit to form knot. Deep fry in hot oil at 350 degrees until golden brown on both sides. Drain on paper towels. Dust with powdered sugar.

Avalanche Lily Seafood Omelette

"A nice Christmas breakfast especially if you serve with country potatoes and home baked breakfast muffin." —James Sproatt, **Mt. Rainier Guest Services,** Ashford

3 lg. EGGS
1 oz. POACHED SALMON, flaked
1 oz. CRAB MEAT
2 oz. SWISS CHEESE, shredded
1 oz. PARMESAN CHEESE
1 oz. TOMATO, diced
1 oz. GREEN ONION, chopped
3 each BAY SHRIMP, for garnish

Make omelette in usual manner adding salmon, crab and Swiss cheese. Fold omelette onto a plate and garnish with parmesan, tomatoes, onion and shrimp.

A Medley of Cheeses

"Christmas is a family event at the Inn. With lights blazing and the table groaning with special treats, it is a real Victorian Christmas." —Barbara DeFreygas, **North Garden Inn Bed & Breakfast,** Bellingham

1 doz. EGGS
1 1/2 cups MILK
1/2 cup BISQUICK®
SALT & PEPPER to taste
1 cup CHEDDAR CHEESE, grated
1/2 cup MONTEREY JACK CHEESE, grated
1/2 cup PARMESAN CHEESE

Combine eggs, milk, bisquick and seasonings; pour into greased 9 x 13 pan. Sprinkle with cheeses. Bake at 350 degrees for 40 minutes until golden around edges and center is firm.

Banana Pecan Pancakes

"This batter is wonderfully versatile. In this recipe, the bananas and pecans give a distinctively appealing texture and flavor."—Laurie Anderson, **Shelburne Country Inn,** Seaview

2 BANANAS	1/2 tsp. SALT
2 EGGS	1 cup CORN MEAL
3 cups BUTTERMILK	1/2 cup BRAN
3 Tbsp. BUTTER	1 Tbsp. HONEY
2 cups UNBLEACHED FLOUR	1/2 cup PECANS
1 tsp. BAKING SODA	

In a medium mixing bowl, mash bananas with fork until lumps are mostly worked out. Add eggs, buttermilk and melted butter; mix thoroughly. In separate bowl, sift flour with baking soda and salt. Stir in bran and corn meal; add dry ingredients to banana mixture stirring until moistened. Add honey and pecans (that have been sautéed in butter until golden). Prepare as any other pancake.

Cranberry Orange Sauce

2 cups SUGAR
1 1/2 cups WATER
24 oz. FRESH CRANBERRIES
1 stick CINNAMON
1/2 cup DRY WHITE WINE
juice and grated rind of 1 ORANGE

Add sugar to water; bring to boil. Add remaining ingredients; bring back to boil and then lower heat to simmer. Simmer 15 to 20 minutes. Remove cinnamon stick and strain mixture, reserving liquid. Place sieved ingredients into a food processor and process one minute. Pour this mixture and the reserved liquid into a saucepan, along with the cinnamon stick and simmer 15 minutes more to thicken. Serve warm over pancakes.

Chapter Seven

Stir Up Sunday

"Stir Up Sunday" is the English name for the Sunday before Advent. By English tradition, it is the last day when you can start stirring up puddings and cakes if they are to be ready for Christmas. Stir Up Sunday does not fall on the same day each year, but always occurs within the last half of November.

What fun it must have been, as the whole family took turns stirring up the pudding, and in turn, making a wish. Then, a coin would be mixed in, along with a ring and a thimble. It is said that the coin would bring worldly goods, the ring a marriage and the thimble a life of being blessed.

Plum porridge was the forerunner of plum pudding, and being similar to mince pies, was originally made with meat. One early porridge recipe informs us that cooks of yesteryear added sugar, raisins, currants, prunes, cochineal, cinnamon and cloves. Brown bread was added as a thickening.

A cheery Scandinavian and English custom in days gone by was the tradition of burning the yule log throughout the holidays to protect and bring good luck to the home.

Kissing under the mistletoe is another tradition originating with the English. The mistletoe tells us that animosities are forgotten, so therefore "kiss and make up." However, you must be careful for as legend tells us, the mistletoe must be burned on the Twelfth Night - or those who kissed under it will never wed.

Many savory and tempting Christmas delights have come from England. The steaming hot mince pies (try the recipe on page 91), rich, dark fruitcakes and flaming plum puddings all are of English origin. The *Dundee Fruitcake* (page 87) is a great tasting version of a longtime, traditional favorite, wonderful for gift-giving and for serving to friends and family!

Hark! The Herald Angels Sing

Hark! The herald angels sing,
Glory to the newborn King!
Peace on Earth, and mercy mild,
God and sinners reconciled!
Joyful, all ye nations rise!
Join the triumph of the skies!
With th'angelic host proclaim,
Christ is born in Bethlehem!
    (Refrain)
Hark! The herald angels sing,
Glory to the newborn King!
Christ, by highest heav'n adored,
Christ, the everlasting Lord!
Late in time, behold him come,
Offspring of the virgin womb!
Veiled in flesh the Godhead see!
Hail th'incarnate Deity!
Pleased as man with man to dwell,
Jesus our Immanuel!
    (Refrain)
Mild he lays his glory by,
Born that man no more may die,
Born to raise the sons of Earth,
Born to give them second birth.
Ris'n with healing in his wings,
Light and life to all he brings!
Hail, the son of righteousness!
Hail the heav'nborn prince of peace!
    (Refrain)

Desserts

Almond Cheesecake

2 (8 oz. pkgs.) CREAM CHEESE, softened
3/4 cup SUGAR
dash SALT
3 EGGS
1/2 tsp. ALMOND EXTRACT

Topping:
   1 cup SOUR CREAM
   5 Tbsp. SUGAR
   1/2 tsp. VANILLA
   1/4 tsp. LEMON RIND, grated
   dash SALT
   TOASTED ALMONDS, chopped, for garnish

Beat together cream cheese, sugar and salt in mixer at medium high speed until fluffy. Add eggs, one at a time, beating after each addition. Add almond extract. Pour in 9 inch pie plate, bake in preheated 325 degree oven for 25 minutes. Remove, cool 20 minutes. Meanwhile, combine sour cream, sugar, vanilla, rind and salt with mixer on low speed. Spread over cheesecake, bake in 350 degree for 15 minutes. Cool; garnish with almonds.

Popcorn Cake

"Every year for Christmas, my mother made this. She would place it on the side bar for snacking."—Marilyn Tatham, Snohomish

3/4 cup BUTTER or MARGARINE, melted
1 1/2 lbs. MARSHMALLOWS, cut in quarters
6 qts. POPPED CORN
1 cup WALNUTS
GUM DROPS, to taste, cut up

Melt butter with marshmallows and pour into popped corn. Butter hands and mix in walnuts and gum drops. Press into buttered tube pan. Red and green gum drops are nice Christmas touches.

Easy Cheesy Lemon Bars

1 pkg. (17 oz.) LEMON CAKE MIX
1/2 cup BUTTER OR MARGARINE, melted
1 EGG, slightly beaten
1 pkg. (13-1/2 oz.) LEMON FROSTING MIX
1 pkg. (8 oz.) CREAM CHEESE, softened
2 EGGS

Combine cake mix, melted butter and one egg. Mix with fork until moist; pat into 9 x 13 inch pan (grease on bottom only). Blend frosting mix into cream cheese; reserve half cup of cheese and frosting mixture. Add 2 eggs to remaining frosting mixture; beat 3 to 5 minutes. Spread over cake mixture; bake at 350 degrees for 30 to 40 minutes. Cool; spread with reserved frosting mixture.

Chocolate Espresso Mousse

Turtleback Farm Inn—*Eastsound, Orcas Island*

4 oz. SEMISWEET CHOCOLATE
  or 3/4 cup CHOCOLATE CHIPS
1/4 cup STRONG ESPRESSO, may use instant espresso
1/2 cup BUTTER
6 Tbsp. SUGAR
3 lg. EGGS

Over low heat, in small heavy saucepan, melt chocolate with espresso. Meanwhile, cut butter into small pieces and put in the bowl of food processor fitted with metal blade. Process butter with sugar until fulffy, about 1 minute. Add warm, melted chocolate espresso mixture. Process 15 seconds; scrape sides of bowl and process again about 20 seconds. Add eggs, one at a time; process for 15 seconds with each addition. Divide mousse into individual serving dishes, and refrigerate until well chilled, at least 4 hours.

White Fruitcake for Christmas

"I first tasted this cake after marrying into the Webb family in 1940. It is an excellent fruitcake."—Marie Webb, Everett

8 EGGS, separated
2 oz. CANDIED ORANGE PEEL
1/2 lb. CANDIED CHERRIES
1/2 lb. CANDIED PINEAPPLE
1 lb. WHITE RAISINS
1 pkg. CANDIED FRUIT MIX

1 lb. BROKEN WALNUTS
1/2 cup APRICOT NECTAR
1 lb. BUTTER
1 lb. POWDERED SUGAR
3 cups FLOUR

Combine candied fruits, raisins, fruit mix and nuts. Pour nectar over all; stir together and let stand. Cream together butter and powdered sugar; add egg yolks. Combine creamed mixture with fruit mixture; mix in flour. Beat egg whites until stiff; combine with mixture. Grease and line with wax paper, five 1 pound coffee cans. Divide batter evenly among the cans. Bake 2 1/2 hours at 275 degrees.

Fresh Apple Cake

*"This cake is so delicious. It is irrestible all by itself, or with a cream cheese frosting or a glaze. Be ready to give the recipe to whomever you serve." — Juanita Warber, **Ocean Crest Resort**, Moclips*

4 cups APPLES, diced
2 cups SUGAR
1/2 cup OIL
2 EGGS, well beaten
2 tsp. VANILLA

2 cups FLOUR
2 tsp. BAKING SODA
2 tsp. CINNAMON
1 tsp. SALT

Lightly spray 9 x 13 pan. Mix all together on low speed of mixer, place in pan and bake one hour in preheated 350 degree oven.

Steamed Holiday Pudding

1 1/2 cups FLOUR, sifted
1 1/2 tsp. BAKING SODA
1 1/2 cups SUGAR
3/4 tsp. SALT
1 1/2 tsp. CLOVES
1 1/2 tsp. CINNAMON
1 1/2 tsp. NUTMEG
3 Tbsp BUTTER, melted
3 EGGS, well beaten
1 1/2 cups RAW CARROTS, grated
1 1/2 cups RAW POTATOES, grated
1 1/2 cups WALNUTS, coarsely chopped
1 1/2 cups RAISINS

Sift flour with dry ingredients; gradually stir butter into eggs in large bowl. Stir in flour mixture and remaining ingredients; mix well. Spoon into buttered 1 1/2 qt. mold, and cover securely with aluminum foil, place lid on top. Place pudding mold on bottom of large pot, pour boiling water 2/3 up the mold. Cover, steam (simmer) for 2 hours. Let rest 2 to 3 minutes, then turn out and serve warm with **Hard Sauce.** Pudding may be wrapped in foil when cool, put in refrigerator and reheated in oven at 350 degrees.

Hard Sauce

1/2 cup BUTTER, softened
1 1/2 cups POWDERED
    SUGAR, sifted
1 EGG YOLK

2 Tbsp. HALF AND HALF
1/8 tsp. SALT
1 tsp. VANILLA
2 Tbsp. BRANDY OR RUM

Cream butter; gradually add sugar. Add slightly beaten egg yolk; stir in cream and flavorings. Beat until creamy. Will keep in refrigerator two weeks. Spoon cold sauce over warm steamed pudding. (Good on gingerbread, too!)

Bavarian Apple Strudel

"This flaky strudel is also most delicious when made with cherry pie filling, and adds color for the season."—Betty Frain, Leavenworth

1 Tbsp. OIL
1 EGG, beaten
1/3 cup LUKEWARM WATER
1/4 tsp. SALT
1 1/2 cups FLOUR
1 cup RAISINS
8 cups TART APPLES, sliced, pared
1/4 cup SUGAR
1 tsp. CINNAMON
1/3 cup BUTTER, melted
1/3 cup DRY BREAD CRUMBS
POWDERED SUGAR

Combine first four ingredients; gradually add flour, beating with spoon until it is a firm dough that pulls away from the sides of the bowl. Knead dough on floured surface until smooth and elastic. Cover, let rest 30 minutes. Combine raisins, apples, sugar and cinnamon and set aside. Divide dough in half; roll each into 18 x 12 rectangle, stretching dough if necessary to make it very thin. Brush with melted butter, sprinkle dough with half of bread crumbs. Spread half of apple mixture lengthwise in center 1/3 of dough. Fold dough over apples on one side and then the other. Brush with melted butter, place on greased baking sheet. Repeat procedure with remaining dough and filling. Bake in 400 degree oven for 30 minutes, until golden brown and apples are tender. Sprinkle with powdered sugar.

Christmas Fruit Crisp

North Garden Inn Bed & Breakfast, *Bellingham*

1 cup CRANBERRIES
2 cups BLUEBERRIES
2 cups APPLES, cored, chopped
1 1/2 cups SUGAR
1 tsp. CINNAMON

Topping:
  1 cup GRANOLA
  1/2 cup NUTS, chopped
  2 Tbsp. BUTTER, melted
  1/2 tsp. CINNAMON
  dash NUTMEG
  VANILLA YOGURT, for garnish

Combine fruit with sugar and cinnamon; pour into greased 9 x 13 pan. Combine topping ingredients; mix together and place on top of fruit. Bake at 350 degrees for 35 to 40 minutes. Garnish with dollop of yogurt.

Cranberry Muffin Cake

North Garden Inn Bed & Breakfast, *Bellingham*

2 1/4 cups FLOUR
1/2 cup SUGAR
1/2 cup PECANS, chopped
1 tsp. BAKING POWDER
1 cup TART APPLE, peeled,
  cored, chopped

1/2 cup BUTTER, melted
3/4 cup MILK
1 EGG
1 tsp. VANILLA
1 cup CRANBERRIES,
  coarsely chopped

In a large bowl, sift dry ingredients together. In medium bowl, combine apple, butter, milk, egg, vanilla and cranberries. Stir into dry ingredients; pour into greased 9 inch round pan. Bake at 400 degrees for 35 to 40 minutes.

Strawberry Supreme

"In this recipe, you may substitute lemon juice and rind for the orange, and use any type of fresh berry. The sauce is also good served over a slice of angel food cake." —Susan Fletcher, **Turtleback Farm Inn,** *Eastsound, Orcas Island*

2 cups STRAWBERRIES, washed, hulled, cut in half
1 Tbsp. SUGAR
1/2 cup SUGAR
2 tsp. ORANGE RIND, grated
1/2 cup ORANGE JUICE
1 cup HEAVY CREAM, whipped

Place strawberries in small bowl; sprinkle with 1 Tbsp. sugar. In a small saucepan, combine 1/2 cup sugar, with orange juice and orange rind; bring to boil. Stir until sugar dissolves; then gently simmer without stirring for about 10 minutes. Let cool completely. To serve, whip cream and fold in orange syrup. Place berries in individual serving bowls and add a generous spoonful of orange cream on top of each.

Celebration Chocolate Chip Pie

1 (9 in.) PIE SHELL, unbaked
2 EGGS
1 cup SUGAR
1/4 cup BUTTER , melted
3 to 4 Tbsp. VANILLA
1/4 cup CORNSTARCH
1 cup PECANS, finely chopped
1 pkg. (6 oz.) CHOCOLATE CHIPS

Prepare pastry shell and set aside. Beat eggs slightly; gradually add sugar. Add melted butter and vanilla; mix well. Blend in cornstarch; stir in pecans and chocolate chips. Pour into unbaked pie shell; bake at 350 degrees for 45 to 50 minutes. Cool one hour before serving.

Chocolate Nut Cake

3/4 cup SHORTENING
2 cups SUGAR
4 sq. CHOCOLATE, melted
4 EGGS
2 1/2 cups FLOUR
1 tsp. BAKING SODA
1 tsp. SALT
1 cup BUTTERMILK
1/2 cup NUTS, chopped
1 tsp. VANILLA

Cream shortening and sugar well. Melt chocolate and add to creamed mixture. Add eggs, one at a time, mixing well after each. Sift together flour, soda and salt; add alternately with buttermilk. Stir in nuts and vanilla. Bake in two 9 inch layer pans at 350 degrees for about 30 minutes. Frost with **Quick Chocolate Icing.**

Quick Chocolate Icing

4 Tbsp. SHORTENING
2 Tbsp. BUTTER
3 sq. CHOCOLATE
5 cups POWDERED SUGAR, divided
1 EGG WHITE
1/2 tsp. SALT
1 tsp. VANILLA
3 to 4 Tbsp. BOILING WATER

Melt shortening, butter and chocolate; cool slightly and stir in 1/2 cup powdered sugar. Add unbeaten egg white, salt, and vanilla; then, remaining powdered sugar. Add hot water a little at a time, just until icing is spreadable.

Dundee Fruitcake

"During the Christmas holidays, serve slices of this old English cake with your favorite hot beverage."—June McGlothlin, *Silver Lake*

1 cup BUTTER or MARGARINE
1 cup SUGAR
5 EGGS
1 tsp. BAKING SODA
1 tsp. MILK
2 1/2 cups FLOUR
1/8 tsp. SALT
3/4 cup CURRANTS
3/4 cup RAISINS
3/4 cup MIXED CANDIED FRUITS
8 RED CANDIED CHERRIES, cut in half
1/2 cup ALMONDS, ground
2 Tbsp. ORANGE PEEL, grated
1/3 cup WHOLE BLANCHED ALMONDS

Cream together butter and sugar until light and fluffy. Add eggs, one at a time, beating after each addition. Dissolve baking soda in milk; add to creamed mixture. Sift together flour and salt, reserve small amount to dredge fruit. Gradually add dry ingredients to creamed mixture, blending well after each addition. Combine fruits, ground almonds, orange peel and reserved flour; mix well. Stir into batter. Spread batter in greased and floured 8 inch springform pan. Arrange whole almonds in circles on top of batter. Bake at 300 degrees, 90 minutes, or until cake tests done. Cool in pan on rack 5 minutes. Remove outer rim and cool completely.

Pistachio Dessert

2 cups RITZ® CRACKERS, crushed
1 cube MARGARINE
2 (3 oz. pkgs.) INSTANT PISTACHIO PUDDING
2 1/2 cups MILK
2 cups VANILLA ICE CREAM, softened
WHIPPED TOPPING
1 CHOCOLATE BAR, grated

Mix crackers and margarine; pat in 9 x 13 inch pan and set aside. Mix pudding with milk, beat until thick. Add ice cream. Pour over crackers and frost with layer of whipped topping. Sprinkle with grated chocolate bar. Will keep refrigerated for 3 to 4 days.

Fresh Pumpkin Pie

"This was my Grandma's recipe. She used canned pumpkin, but I prefer using freshly cooked. It makes a world of difference."—Jennifer Knudson, Mukilteo

4 EGGS
1 cups SUGAR
1/2 cup BROWN SUGAR
1/2 tsp. SALT
2 1/2 tsp. CINNAMON
2 tsp. GINGER
1 1/4 tsp. NUTMEG
4 cups FRESHLY COOKED PUMPKIN
1 cup MILK
1 lg. can EVAPORATED MILK
2 (9 in.) UNBAKED PIE SHELLS

Beat eggs well, adding sugar, salt and spices. Stir in pumpkin until well mixed. Pour in milk; combine well. Pour into pie shell and bake at 400 degrees for 45 to 60 minutes.

Pumpkin Chiffon Pie

"This pie is so light, our guests devour it, even after an enormous Holiday meal. Garnish as desired; then enjoy a little slice of heaven."—**Mio Amore Pensione,** *Trout Lake*

1 can (29 oz.) PUMPKIN
3/4 cup MILK
1 1/2 cups BROWN SUGAR, packed
1/8 tsp. SALT
1/2 tsp. GINGER
1 tsp. CINNAMON
1/3 tsp. NUTMEG
5 EGGS, separated, whites beaten until stiff
2 env. UNFLAVORED GELATIN
2/3 cup COLD WATER
1 1/2 cups HEAVY CREAM
1/3 cup SUGAR
2 (8 or 9 in.) BAKED, COOLED PIE SHELLS

In top of double boiler, combine pumpkin, milk, brown sugar, salt and spices. Heat until sugar is dissolved and thoroughly mixed. Place beaten egg yolks in a bowl; stir in 1/2 cup hot mixture. Add egg yolk mixture to hot mixture in double boiler. Cook, stirring constantly, until thickened. Soften gelatin in small bowl in cold water. Stir into pumpkin mixture; remove from heat. Let stand to cool; stirring occasionally. Blend in beaten egg whites; chill mixture until partially set (1 to 1/2 hours). Do not let set fully. In separate bowl, combine heavy cream and sugar and whip until stiff. Blend into pumpkin mixture; pour into baked pie shells. Refrigerate until set. Garnish.

Holiday Chiffon Pie

"This recipe was given to me by a friend many years ago. It has become a family favorite. I prefer making it the day it is to be served."—Jimmie Holeman, Anacortes

3 EGGS, separated
1/2 cup SUGAR
1/2 cup PUMPKIN
1/2 cup MILK
1/2 tsp. GINGER
1/2 tsp. NUTMEG
1/2 tsp. CINNAMON
1/2 tsp. SALT
1/4 cup WATER
1 env. UNFLAVORED
  GELATIN
1/2 cup SUGAR
BAKED PIE SHELL
WHIPPED CREAM

Beat yolks; add 1/2 cup sugar, pumpkin, milk, spices and salt. Cook until thick. Meanwhile, in the water, soften gelatin. Stir into hot mixture; cool. Beat egg whites with remaining sugar until stiff; fold into cooled pumpkin mixture. Pour into shell and chill. Garnish with whipped cream. If desired, may increase pumpkin to 1 1/4 cups.

Chocolate Pie

"This recipe is from my 1942 8th grade cooking class. It uses no eggs, because at the time, eggs were rationed. My granddaughter makes this recipe now for our family holidays. It is a MUST!"— Evelyn Hayes, Lakewood

1 sq. CHOCOLATE
1/2 cup SUGAR
1 3/4 cup MILK
1/2 tsp. SALT
1/4 cup CORNSTARCH
1/4 cup MILK
1/2 tsp. VANILLA
WHIPPED CREAM
CHOPPED NUTS
8 inch BAKED PIE SHELL

Melt the chocolate; add sugar, milk and salt; stir until dissolved. Combine cornstarch and milk; add to chocolate mixture. Cook, stirring, until thick; add vanilla. Let cool. Pour into baked pie shell; top with whipped cream and nuts.

Cranberry Cherry Pie

"Pretty in color, unusual in flavor."—Iona Durnan, Yakima

1 can (21 oz.) CHERRY PIE FILLING
1 can (16 oz.) WHOLE BERRY CRANBERRY SAUCE
1/2 cup GOLDEN OR DARK SEEDLESS RAISINS
2 Tbsp. CORNSTARCH
1/4 tsp. GINGER
1 pkg. (10 to 11 oz.) PIE CRUST MIX
5 to 7 Tbsp. ORANGE JUICE
MILK
SUGAR

In large bowl, stir cherry pie filling, cranberry sauce, raisins, cornstarch and ginger. Set aside while you prepare pie crust mix as label directs for 2 crust pie, but substitute orange juice for water. Divide pastry into two pieces. Roll on lightly floured surface and gently ease pastry into pie plate. Spoon filling into pie crust. Roll remaining pastry for top crust, into 12 inch round. Cut into 14 strips. Weave strips into a lattice; seal ends. Make high fluted edge; brush pastry with milk, sprinkle lightly with sugar. Bake in preheated 400 degree oven for 50 minutes until fruit mixture begins to bubble and crust is golden.

Crumble Top Mincemeat Pie

1 cup COCONUT, shredded
1/3 cup BROWN SUGAR
1/2 cup NUTS, chopped
2 Tbsp. BUTTER

1 jar PREPARED MINCE-MEAT
1 (9 inch) UNBAKED PIE SHELL

Make your favorite pastry for pie crust. Reserve 1/3 cup, firmly packed, for topping. Crumble reserved pastry mix to size of peas, combine with coconut, brown sugar, nuts and butter. Place mincemeat in prepared shell and sprinkle with topping. Bake at 400 degrees, 20 to 25 minutes.

Mincemeat Chiffon Pie

"My Dad insisted on having mincemeat pie at Christmas, but all of us five kids didn't care for it. So Mom came up with this version that much lightens and sweetens the mincemeat. She didn't leave us the recipe, but I have come as close as memory permits." — Simone Nichols, **Groveland Cottage**, Sequim

1 env. UNFLAVORED GELATIN
2/3 cup SUGAR, divided
1/2 tsp. SALT
1/4 cup WATER
3 EGGS, separated
1/2 cup COINTREAU
1 1/4 cup PREPARED MINCEMEAT
1/2 cup HEAVY CREAM, whipped
CANDIED CHERRIES, if desired
1 BAKED PIE CRUST

In top part of small double boiler, mix gelatin, 1/3 cup sugar and salt. Stir in water; then beat in egg yolks one at a time. Add the cointreau and cook over simmering water stirring constantly until gelatin dissolves and mixture in slightly thickened. Remove from heat; stir in mincemeat and cool. Beat egg whites until stiff but not dry. Gradually add remaining 1/3 cup sugar and beat until very stiff. Fold in gelatin mixture and whipped cream; pile lightly into cold crust and chill until firm. Decorate with more whipped cream and candied cherries, if desired. A crumb crust works nicely, too.

Double Layered Pumpkin Pie

"I made this for Christmas, and it was a super hit with my nephew and his wife. Now, it has become a tradition at their home."—Joyce Fowler, Puyallup

1 (3 oz. pkg.) CREAM CHEESE, softened
1 Tbsp. HALF AND HALF
1 Tbsp. SUGAR
1 1/2 cups NON-DAIRY WHIPPED TOPPING
GRAHAM CRACKER CRUMB CRUST
1 cup HALF AND HALF
2 sm. pkgs. VANILLA INSTANT PUDDING
1 (16 oz. can) PUMPKIN
1 tsp. CINNAMON
1/2 tsp. GINGER
1/4 tsp. CLOVES

Mix cream cheese, 1 Tbsp. half and half, and sugar until smooth. Gently stir in topping; spread over bottom of crust. Pour remaining half and half in mixing bowl; add pudding mix. Beat with wire whip until well blended; let stand 5 minutes or until thickened. Stir in pumpkin and spices mixing well. Spread over cream cheese layer; refrigerate overnight. Garnish with additional whipped topping if desired.

Cherry Mini-Cheesecakes

24 VANILLA WAFERS
1 lb. CREAM CHEESE
3/4 cup SUGAR
2 EGGS
1 tsp. VANILLA
1 can CHERRY PIE FILLING

Fill 24 muffin cups with cupcake liners; add wafers to liners. Beat cream cheese, sugar, eggs and vanilla together; fill liners about half full. Bake at 350 degrees for 15 minutes; cool. Add 2 or 3 spoonsful of cherry pie filling on top.

Cream Cheese Cupcakes

"My birthday is Christmas Day. Instead of birthday cake, my Mom always makes these, my favorite cupcakes."—Jana Hawkins, Bellingham

8 oz. CREAM CHEESE, softened
1 EGG
1/3 cup SUGAR
1/8 tsp. SALT
1 (6 oz. bag) CHOCOLATE CHIPS

Batter:
    1 1/2 cups FLOUR
    1 cup SUGAR
    1 tsp. BAKING SODA
    1/4 cup COCOA
    1/2 tsp. SALT
    1 cup WATER
    1/3 cup OIL
    1 Tbsp. VINEGAR
    1 tsp. VANILLA

Combine cream cheese, egg, sugar and salt; should be very warm. Add chocolate chips and set aside. Blend all batter ingredients; spoon into cupcake liners in muffin tins. Place 1 Tbsp. of cream cheese mixture in the center of each. Bake at 350 degrees for 25 to 30 minutes.

The Twelfth Night Cake

The early tradition of the Twelfth Night cake began with the notion of putting beans in a cake. Later, the English put a coin in the mixture instead. At first, a silver farthing was used, later a penny, and still later, a threepenny bit. Whoever found the coin was assured good luck in the coming year.

Devonshire Cream with Crimson Sauce

*"This recipe is served at our annual Christmas brunch."—Phyllis Morgan, **Fulton House Bed & Breakfast**, Mt. Vernon*

1 tsp. UNFLAVORED GELATIN
3/4 cup COLD WATER
1 cup WHIPPING CREAM
1/2 cup SUGAR
1 1/2 tsp. VANILLA
1 (8 oz. ctn.) SOUR CREAM

In small saucepan, soften gelatin in water; heat till gelatin dissolves; cool. In a large mixer bowl, beat together cream, sugar and vanilla till soft peaks form (tips curl). Do not over beat; combine gelatin mixture and sour cream and mix well. Fold sour cream mixture into whipped cream; pour whipped mixture into stemmed glasses or dessert dishes; chill. Top with **Crimson Sauce** when ready to serve.

Crimson Sauce

4 tsp. ORANGE PEEL, finely shredded
1/4 cup ORANGE JUICE
2 cups WHOLE FRESH CRANBERRIES, divided
1 1/3 cups WATER
1/2 cup SUGAR

In saucepan, combine the orange peel and juice, 1 1/2 cups cranberries and water. Bring to boiling, reduce heat. Boil gently uncovered for 15 minutes more. Sieve sauce; return to saucepan and add remaining cranberries and sugar. Cook 5 minutes, or until skins pop. Cool; cover and chill.

Chapter Eight

The Holly and the Ivy . . .

Wrapped in the aura of the season, the sparkle of the stars and angels, the richness of reds and greens, and the aromas of evergreens filling each room your home becomes transformed at Christmas. In the waning glow of the evening, family and guests gather to share stories that will be cherished for years to come.

To create a "Christmas scent" in your house, combine in a saucepan the peels of 2 oranges, 3 cinnamon sticks, 12 whole cloves and 2 1/2 cups water. Gently simmer uncovered on the stove and add more water as it evaporates.

 Whether on the sideboard, mantle or included in your centerpiece, candles are another excellent way to add warmth and charm to your celebration.

To conclude your holiday gathering choose from the luscious desserts, cookies and candies featured in this book.

Whether the holidays are celebrated in Washington's cities such as Seattle, Spokane and Tacoma, or in its smaller communities, the many traditions and cultures that formed the Evergreen State make the Christmas season here a treasure of unforgetable memories. We hope this book has given you ideas to incorporate in your holiday celebrations with family and friends.

Candies, Cookies and more . . .

Almond Roca

"This is a chocolate lover's dream, so rich and fresh compared to the roca that is in stores. You'll never buy it again."—Juanita Warber, Ocean Crest Resort, Moclips

1 cup WALNUTS, finely chopped
1 bag (12 oz.) CHOCOLATE CHIPS, divided
2 sticks BUTTER
3/4 cup SUGAR
3/4 cup ALMONDS, slivered, divided

Grease 9 x 9 pan; sprinkle walnuts in pan and one half of chocolate chips. Place in oven on warm and melt. Meanwhile, melt butter in sauce pan; dissolve sugar in butter and add 1/2 cup almonds. Cook until it turns brown in color, about 8 to 10 minutes, using low heat; stir constantly. Pour mixture over warm chocolate and walnuts. Spread quickly (it hardens as it cools). Sprinkle remaining chips and almonds on top; pat down and chill.

Cathedral Windows

1 pkg. (6 oz.) CHOCOLATE CHIPS
1/2 cup BUTTER
1 EGG, well beaten
1 cup POWDERED SUGAR
1 pkg. (10 1/2 oz.) COLORED MINIATURE
**   MARSHMALLOWS**
FINE COCONUT or POWDERED SUGAR

Melt chips in butter in top of double boiler. Cool slightly; add egg. Continue to cool until lukewarm; add sugar and marshmallows and roll in coconut or powdered sugar. Makes three rolls; slice when cool. Keep refrigerated.

"Feliz Navidad" — Merry Christmas in Spanish

Five Minute Fudge

2 Tbsp. BUTTER
2/3 cup EVAPORATED MILK
1 2/3 cup SUGAR
1/2 tsp. SALT
2 cups MINI MARSHMALLOWS
1 1/2 cups CHOCOLATE CHIPS
1 tsp. VANILLA
1/2 cup NUTS, chopped

Combine butter, milk, sugar and salt in saucepan over medium heat; bring to boil. Cook 5 minutes, stirring constantly. (Start timing when mixture starts to bubble around edges of pan.) Remove from heat; stir in marshmallows, chocolate chips, vanilla and nuts. Stir vigorously for 2 minutes, until marshmallows and chips are blended. Pour into 8 inch square buttered pan; cool and enjoy.

Nut Crunch

1 1/4 cups SUGAR
3/4 cup BUTTER or MARGARINE
1 1/4 tsp. SALT
1/4 cup WATER
1/2 cup UNBLANCHED ALMONDS
1/2 tsp. BAKING SODA
1/2 cup BLANCHED ALMONDS
1/2 cup WALNUTS or BRAZIL NUTS, chopped
1/3 cup CHOCOLATE CHIPS, melted
1/2 cup NUTS, finely chopped

Combine first five ingredients in saucepan. Bring to a boil, stirring often. When temperature reaches 290 degrees, or a little dropped in cold water is brittle, remove from heat. Stir in next three ingredients; pour onto greased cookie sheet. Spread with melted chocolate; sprinkle top with remaining nuts. Cool and break up.

Candied Cranberries

"A unique method of using cranberries. It was given to me by a friend, who used this as a substitute for Christmas candy."— Bernice Dye, Everett

CRANBERRIES
2 EGG WHITES
POWDERED SUGAR
WHITE SUGAR

Wash cranberries and pat dry. Whip egg whites, adding a little powdered sugar. Add the cranberries, a handful at a time and coat with the egg white mixture. Place in paper bag with white sugar; shake well until coated. Dry on paper towel.

Caramels

"I have a hard time keeping up with requests for these. It is a great favorite at Christmas."—Vera Rome, Everett

2 cups BROWN SUGAR
1 cup DARK CORN SYRUP
1/2 lb. BUTTER
1 can SWEETENED CONDENSED MILK
1 tsp. VANILLA, optional

Combine all ingredients and cook in heavy pan, stirring constantly. Cook until candy forms very hard ball when dropped in small amount of cold water, about 20 minutes. Pour into 8 x 11 pan and mark into squares when nearly cool. If harder toffee is desired, cook a little longer.

Yule Cookie Logs

"Christmas is a special time for us. We always have guests at Christmas. They are usually relatives of families in our neighborhood. We enjoy helping to make their visit special. These cookies send a special holiday scent throughout the house. Our guests enjoy them with a cup of tea in the afternoon" —Barbie Guay, **Albatross Bed & Breakfast,** Anacortes

3 cups FLOUR
1 tsp. NUTMEG
1 cup BUTTER
2 tsp. VANILLA
2 tsp. RUM FLAVORING
3/4 cup SUGAR
1 EGG, unbeaten

Frosting:
    4 Tbsp. BUTTER
    1/2 tsp. VANILLA
    1 tsp. RUM FLAVORING
    3 cups POWDERED SUGAR, sifted
    3 to 4 Tbsp. CREAM

Sift together flour and nutmeg; cream butter with vanilla and rum flavoring. Gradually add sugar, creaming well. Blend in egg, add dry ingredients gradually and mix well. Shape pieces of dough on lightly floured surface into long rolls, one half inch in diameter. Cut into 3 inch lengths; place on ungreased baking sheet. Bake at 350 degrees for 12 to 15 minutes; cool and frost. Cream butter, vanilla, and rum flavoring; add powdered sugar alternately with cream, beating until spreadable. Mark frosting with tines of fork to resemble a log. Sprinkle with nutmeg.

Merry Christmas in French . . . "Joyeux Noel"

Fruitcake Squares

6 Tbsp. BUTTER, melted
4 cups VANILLA WAFER CRUMBS
3/4 cup CANDIED GREEN CHERRIES
3/4 cup CANDIED RED CHERRIES
1/2 cup CANDIED PINEAPPLE
3/4 cup DATES, chopped
1 cup PECAN HALVES
1 can SWEETENED CONDENSED MILK
1/2 cup BOURBON

Place butter in 15 x 10 x 1 inch pan, sprinkle crumbs on butter. Arrange fruit and nuts on top; press in. Combine milk and bourbon; pour over mixture evenly. Bake at 350 degrees for 20 to 25 minutes. Cool completely; cut in squares.

Food for the Angels

3 EGG WHITES
3/4 cup SUGAR
1 tsp. VANILLA
25 RITZ® CRACKERS, crushed
1 cup NUTS
1 cup WHIPPING CREAM
COCONUT

Beat egg whites until stiff; gradually add sugar and vanilla. Fold in crackers and nuts. Pour into greased 8 x 8 pan; bake at 350 degreees for 20 to 25 minutes. Cool. Whip cream; spread over baked cookies. Sprinkle with coconut; refrigerate overnight. This is really better on second or third day. Cut into squares; serve.

In Russian, "S Rozhestvom Khristovyn" means Merry Christmas!

Chipit Oatmeal Cookies

2 cups FLOUR, sifted
1/2 tsp. SALT
2 cups ROLLED OATS
1/2 cup COCONUT
1 cup SHORTENING
1 cup BROWN SUGAR,
   lightly packed

1 tsp. BAKING SODA
1/4 cup BOILING WATER
1 tsp. VANILLA
1 cup DATES, chopped
CHOPPED NUTS

Stir sifted flour and salt together; mix in oats and coconut and set aside. Cream shortening and sugar well. Dissolve baking soda in boiling water. Gradually stir into creamed mixture; stir in vanilla. Add flour mixture, small amounts at a time, mixing well after each addition. Stir in dates and nuts. Drop dough by small spoonfuls, well apart on greased cookie sheet. Flatten each mound with glass, dipped in flour. Bake at 375 degrees for eight minutes. May substitute chocolate chips for dates, if desired.

Danish Christmas Cookies

1 cup BUTTER
1/2 cup SUGAR
1/2 tsp. LEMON EXTRACT

1/2 tsp. ALMOND EXTRACT
1/2 tsp. VANILLA
2 1/2 cups FLOUR, sifted

Cream together butter and sugar until light and fluffy. Beat in extracts, gradually stir in flour. Cover with plastic wrap, chill 30 minutes. Shape into 13 inch long roll. Refrigerate 8 hours or overnight; cut in 1/4 inch thick slices. Place 2 inches apart on greased baking sheet. Bake in 350 degree oven for 8 minutes until golden brown. Remove, cool on rack and frost with your favorite icing.

In Danish . . . "Glaedelig Jul" . . . Merry Christmas!

Triple Layer Cookie Bars

1/2 cup BUTTER OR MARGARINE
1 1/2 cups GRAHAM CRACKER CRUMBS
1 pkg. (7 oz.) COCONUT
1 can SWEETENED CONDENSED MILK
1 pkg. (12 oz.) CHOCOLATE CHIPS
1/2 cup CREAMY PEANUT BUTTER

Preheat oven to 350 degrees. In 9 x 13 pan, melt butter in oven; sprinkle crumbs evenly over butter. Top with coconut, and then milk. Bake 25 minutes until lightly brown. In small pan, melt chips and peanut butter. Spread over hot coconut, cool and chill thoroughly.

Shortbread Cookies

"A delightful variety of shortbread."—Vera Rome, Everett

1 cup BUTTER
1 tsp. VANILLA
1/2 cup GRANULATED SUGAR
1/2 cup COCONUT, fine, unsweetened
1 cup FLOUR
2 cups ROLLED OATS

Combine ingredients and form long rolls. Keep in refrigerator several hours. Slice 1/2 inch thick; bake at 325 degrees until brown (15 minutes).

Index

About the Author

For as long as she can remember, **Janet Walker** has had a passion for cooking. She loves experimenting with recipes and collecting recipes from other cooks.

A mother of three and grandmother to four, Janet resides in the Evergreen City of Everett, Washington, north of metropolitan Seattle.

Her parents moved from Tulsa, Oklahoma to Anacortes when she was only eight years old. In this beautiful city on Fidalgo Island, she met and married her husband, Ivan. They have been married for over 40 years.

Janet's first work for Golden West Publishers was the **Washington Cook Book,** which has been highly successful. She was next assigned to author a cook book for our neighboring state. Entitled the **Oregon Cook Book** it, too, has been well received!

Janet's love for cooking has prompted her to create yet another cook book. "There are so many special dishes that are unique to the Holiday Season," she says. This book features the delectable recipes found here in the great state of Washington. Many of the recipes have been contributed by some of Washington's finest bed and breakfast inns, and from many other cooks throughout the state.

To her readers, Janet says, "Add your own special personal touches to the recipes found here. Cooking need not be a chore, make it fun! Let others assist in the preparation and serving. I know these dishes will add that *special touch* to your Holiday meals."

Christmas Cook Books
from Golden West Publishers

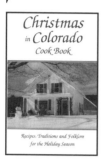

CHRISTMAS IN COLORADO COOK BOOK

Christmas holiday traditions, folklore and favorite foods from the Rockies. Includes recipes from innkeepers, homemakers, and professional chefs. Wide variety of flavors, from *Olde English Plum Pudding* to *Denver Frittatas*.

5 1/2 x8 1/2—120 pages . . . $8.95

CHRISTMAS IN ARIZONA COOK BOOK

'Tis the season . . . celebrate Christmas in sunny Arizona. Read about the fascinating southwestern traditions and foods. Create a southwestern holiday spirit with this wonderful cook book. By Lynn Nusom.

6 x 9—128 pages . . . $8.95

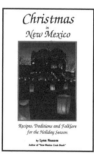

CHRISTMAS IN NEW MEXICO COOK BOOK

Recipes, traditions and folklore for the Holiday Season—or all year long. Try *Three Kings Bread, Posole de Posada, Christmas Pumpkin Pie, Christmas Turkey with White Wine Basting Sauce,* and many more taste tempters! Makes an excellent gift! By Lynn Nusom.

6 x 9—144 pages . . . $8.95

CHRISTMAS IN TEXAS COOK BOOK

Multi-cultural recipes that reflect the numerous ethnic influences of this great state. Try *Festive Mexican Pizza, Pasta Siciliana, Squash Dressing Casserole, Black Forest Cherry Cake* and *Cowboy Cookies*. Texas folklore and traditions. Enjoy the spirit and warmth that is so uniquely Texas!

5 1/2 x 8 1/2 — 120 pages . . . $8.95

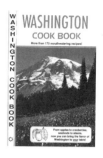

ORDER BLANK

GOLDEN WEST PUBLISHERS

☼ 4113 N. Longview Ave. • Phoenix, AZ 85014

602-265-4392 • **1-800-658-5830** • FAX 602-279-6901

Qty	Title	Price	Amount
	Apple Lovers Cook Book	5.95	
	Chili-Lovers' Cook Book	5.95	
	Chip and Dip Lovers Cook Book	5.95	
	Christmas in Arizona Cook Book	8.95	
	Christmas in Colorado Cook Book	8.95	
	Christmas in New Mexico Cook Book	8.95	
	Christmas in Texas Cook Book	8.95	
	Christmas in Washington Cook Book	8.95	
	Easy RV Recipes	6.95	
	Easy Recipes for Wild Game & Fish	6.95	
	Joy of Muffins	5.95	
	Oregon Cook Book	5.95	
	Pecan Lovers Cook Book	6.95	
	Pumpkin Lovers Cook Book	6.95	
	Quick-n-Easy Mexican Recipes	5.95	
	Salsa Lovers Cook Book	5.95	
	Tequila Cook Book	7.95	
	Veggie Lovers Cook Book	6.95	
	Washington Cook Book	5.95	
	Wholly Frijoles! The Whole Bean Cook Book	6.95	
	Add $2.00 to total order for shipping & handling	**$2.00**	

☐ My Check or Money Order Enclosed. . . . . $ _____

☐ MasterCard   ☐ VISA   (Payable in U.S. funds)

Acct. No. _____   Exp. Date _____

Signature _____

Name _____   Telephone _____

Address _____

City/State/Zip _____

Call or write for FREE catalog

10/95   MasterCard and VISA Orders Accepted ($20 Minimum)

X Wash